BOOK SIX

The Book We Call The Bible

Enjoying The Best That Life Has To Offer
With
Kenneth W. Howard, PhD

Published By
Direction Inc.
Established 1974
Middletown, Ohio

Direction, Inc.
PO Box 213
Middletown, Ohio 45042
e-mail   direct @ siscom.net

Web address: http://www.answersandmore.com

First printing 2002
ISBN: 0-9703777-1-1
Library of Congress Control Number: 2001118541

Printed in the United States of America
Evangel Press
Nappanee, Indiana

Our acknowledgement and thanks to the NASA space program for the remarkable photographs of our universe and solar system that helped in the design of this book cover. Through the efforts of NASA we are privileged to enjoy a more intimate glimpse into God's remarkable creation.

Contents

(More contents next page)

Some Interesting Facts About The Bible That You May Not Have Heard Before

Hi, I'm Ken Howard

You and I are family. We may not have the same last name or come from the same country, but we're still family. We live together on this planet called earth and someday soon we'll venture on to another life. That fact alone makes us family ...and puts us on the same common ground.

You and I also have questions that we want answered... but we want the real facts and truth. The problem is...there are a lot of conflicting philosophies floating around out there that could make a person wonder if there is any real truth to be found anywhere. But that's not a problem, as you will soon learn.

This is your life and my life we're dealing with here, and we want to make sure that we have the correct information so that you and I can make the best decisions for our life as we possibly can.

That's why this little book was written. It was written for you...just because you're worth the effort. I hope you will find it helpful in your pursuit toward enjoying the very best that life has to offer. The good thing about life is...life can be a good thing. Enjoy!

THE GOOD NEWS
AND
THE BAD NEWS

To the surprise of many people, the Bible is not a book about religion…it is a book about life. The Bible stands alone as the single authority to define who we are, where we came from, why we exist and where we are ultimately headed.

No other writing in all of human history compares to the wisdom and authority of the Bible…the reason being, the Bible is authored by the omniscient Creator of the universe, who has graciously provided His eternal truths so that you and I may enjoy the very best that life has to offer (now and forever).

All areas of scholarly research continue to confirm the validity and accuracy of the Bible. Those who take a serious approach to the Bible acknowledge it as a genuine miracle.

No book or writing has been more controversial than the Bible. From the moment it arrived, the Bible has been exposed to continual conflict from those who chose to deny its authority and credibility. To deny God, you first must deny the Bible!

Opposing religions have tried to discredit it; political empires have tried to physically destroy it from the face of the earth; philosophers have offered contrasting theories; scientists have tried to challenge its principles of physics and chemistry; and multitudes of oblivious and preoccupied individuals simply choose to ignore it. Yet the Bible remains intact!

The question one has to ask is "why?" Why have there been so many attacks and efforts to dismiss this book and its teachings? Why have kings ordered all copies of it burned? Why have religious leaders outlawed the reading of it? Why do people still ignore it while indulging themselves with countless other unproven theories and philosophies? The answer is obvious...a majority of mankind is threatened by its teachings.

Sadly, the Bible has birthed conflicting religious groups who interpret its teachings through the private and political ambitions of man...rather than by the seeking of God's will. For some people, these different religious doctrines call the Bible's integrity into question...but is this being fair to the book?

The history of some religions, that claim the Bible as their spiritual authority, has been less than honorable...to put it mildly. Some religions have used the Bible as their authority for the enslavement and destruction of human bodies and souls. Evil religious leaders have quoted the Bible as their justification for religious wars, mass killings, persecutions and imprisonments.

It is no wonder that many people are confused and ask questions like..."What kind of God would endorse such evil as the Crusades or the Inquisition...which were carried out by those who claim allegiance to the Bible? But, does the Bible endorse such behavior, or have those with evil intentions abused its message? The truth is, the integrity of the Bible is not defined by the actions of those who read it. We must look elsewhere.

Even in all of the confusion, while multitudes try to ignore or challenge its teaching, there are millions of other people who have found the Bible to be a powerful and certain guide toward a successful, fulfilling and happy life...as well as the source of eternal hope. It is this group of people, throughout history, who help to define the purity and integrity of Biblical truth. They have learned to take the Bible at its promise...and their lives have greatly benefited by doing so. The certainty and stability of life is grounded on reality and truth...and only in the Bible are we are assured of finding the truth that endures...

> (Words of Jesus) "You shall know the truth, and the truth shall make you free."   John 8:31-32

BIBLE CREDIBILITY

The Bible has passed all the tests to satisfy the "law of credibility"...withstanding the challenges to its authenticity. It stands alone as the only authority for human life and beyond.

Even so, there are questions that must be answered. How can we be certain that the Bible is the word of our Creator, and not just another piece of old literature? Didn't men write the Bible? Can any of the Bible's ancient teachings be relevant for today's modern society? Why should I trust the Bible to provide real answers and guidance to the daily issues of my life today?

Aren't there errors and contradictions in the Bible? If there is just one Bible, then why are there so many different translations and different interpretations to what it says? How can I find the truth even if I wanted to?

These are questions that demand answers if the Bible is to be taken seriously...for its teachings are of such magnitude and importance that they cannot be ignored. And that's exactly where this writing is headed...to provide you with the evidence to answer those questions.

When you finish reading these next few chapters you will have a better understanding and deeper appreciation of the greatest book ever written...and you'll also realize why every respected scientist and historian on earth stands in awe of this amazing book. Enjoy!

POP QUIZ

Which of the following phrases are found in the Bible and which are not?

(1) A word to the wise is sufficient

(2) In God we trust

(3) God helps those who help themselves

(4) Cleanliness is next to godliness

(5) Practice what you preach

(6) Let your conscience be your guide

(7) Where there's a will, there's a way

Answer…<u>none</u> of these quotations are found in the Bible. But, don't feel bad at your score…many people put words in God's mouth, to quote the Bible erroneously as their supreme authority. But here's some cute stuff the Bible actually does say, even though it sounds like some "old timer" made it up…"the skin of my teeth", "a drop in the bucket", "see eye to eye", "the apple of his eye", "good for nothing", "half dead". Yep, the Bible actually gets the credit for these old-timer sayings.

People today still add and subtract words from the Bible that make a world of difference to the meaning. Some do it in error while others try to add authority to false doctrine. But this isn't something new. Take the "Wicked Bible" for example.

Way back in 1631 AD, there was an edition of the King James Bible that was wrongly printed (just in error). The only problem was, it left out one little word "not" from Exodus 20:14. The printer was fined for his error…but all he did was change the 7th commandment to read, *"Thou shalt commit adultery."* From what's going on in today's world, I'd suspicion this to be the Bible of choice by those of the 1960's "revolting sexual revolution" and the current "do it to whoever will let you" logic.

Although most copies were immediately destroyed by order of Charles I, there are still eleven existing copies of the "Wicked Bible"…one of which is on display at the Bible museum in Branson, Missouri. So, my advice to all you southern folk down yonder in Branson is to "take care what you read".

Apparently, the little word "not" is rather troublesome for our human family. Another printer (1653 AD) just happened to omit it from a "not very good place" in the Bible. It does make a difference in the interpretation when you read the verse in I Corinthians 6: 9 the right way and the wrong way...

> "Know ye not that the unrighteous shall inherit the kingdom of God."...OOOPS.

> "Know ye not that the unrighteous shall <u>not</u> inherit the kingdom of God."

This printing mistake was known as the "Unrighteous Bible" and immediately recalled...much to the dismay of many (unrighteous) people who thought their prayers had finally been answered.

So, what's the point in all this? Sure, there have been errors in printing and interpretation of the Bible, but they do not go unnoticed. Somebody is always watching, and you and I can be assured that the teachings of the book are just exactly what the Creator wanted us to read.

Johannes Gutenberg invented the printing press in 1438 AD. The first book he printed (1454 AD) was the Bible...of which there still exists a significant part of 48 copies of his original 180 printed copies. There were no printing errors in Gutenberg's edition. Same holds true in modern publications.

THE BIBLE'S POPULARITY

Is the Bible a popular book? Consider this...today there are more than five hundred million pieces (500,000,000) of Bible Scripture distributed annually. The Bible is now available in more than two thousand languages (2,233) while current work continues to translate into hundreds of others.

The first translation of the English Bible was during the seventh century, but Anglo-Saxon English was not used the same way it is today. As languages changed, it was the Bible that was first to be translated...showing how important this book has been to former generations.

By the end of the thirteenth century, the Anglo-Saxon language developed into what is known as "Middle English". The John Wyclif Bible was translated from Latin (1388 AD) but it didn't reflect the "new" English language. John Purvey, with some help from others, corrected Wyclif's translation, creating an easier to read translation that remained popular for 100 years.

William Tyndale (1526 AD) completed an English translation of the Erasmus Greek New Testament. He published a translation of the Pentateuch (1530) and selections from the Old Testament (1531). In 1535, Tyndale printed revised editions of his New Testament translations, but much of his work was destroyed because of religious and political opposition. He died while making an English translation of Luther's German.

Miles Coverdale published the first English translation of the entire Bible (1535 AD). Many more English translations came along later, as the language developed and as discoveries of the Bible's origin were better known.

The Geneva Bible (1560); the King James (1611); the American Standard Edition (1901); the Bible in Modern English (1903); Today's English Version (1966); the New International Version (1972) all reveal the ongoing translation process as world languages are used differently. The Bible is now available in more than 2,200 of the 2,700 languages spoken in the world. No other book or writing is so protected, to maintain a current level of communication. For the majority of the world, this book is worth the effort.

TEACHINGS OF THE BIBLE
FAR AHEAD OF ITS TIME

Another remarkable evidence to the divine wisdom of the Bible is in its "scientific" knowledge that precedes human discovery. Keep in mind that the writers were mere humans who had no formal education. The knowledge they disclosed came from God, for no man could have known these truths otherwise.

In the following examples, we see how Biblical writers spoke of things in total conflict to the popular held beliefs and teaching of their day. Of the two choices, the Bible writers chose to record truth rather than the superstitions of their fellowman.

9

Common Belief Of The Day   **Stated Bible Fact**

Common Belief Of The Day	Stated Bible Fact
Disease and spirits reside in blood and the way to cure a disease is to bleed patient.	Blood is essential to life Leviticus 17:11-14
Male alone has the life of the baby in him. The woman is only an incubator.	Both male and female possess "seed of life" Genesis 3:15 and 22:18
Raw human and animal blood was used as a beverage and considered to be healthy.	The drinking of blood is unhealthy and forbidden Leviticus 17:12-14
All animal meat is OK to eat regardless of manner of death.	Animals that died naturally are unhealthy and forbidden to eat Leviticus 17:15
Transmission of contagious disease was not understood. Isolation not practiced.	There is a necessity of quarantine of certain diseases Leviticus 13-15
Everything is suitable to eat. There are no unhealthy foods or restrictions.	Eating of pork and scavengers prohibited (for both religious and health purposes). Leviticus 11
Unaware of the need for basic hygiene or isolation from bacterial contamination.	How to avoid contamination from one another Leviticus 15:19-33
No understanding of need for environmental control. Common practice to pollute ground with human waste.	Practical advice on disposing of human waste products by burying it beneath surface. Deuteronomy 23:12-14
Lack of understanding about relationship of cleanliness to contagion of disease.	Advise on washing oneself and burning of clothes after contact with deceased man or animal Numbers 19:5-22
Belief that the earth is flat.	Earth is round. Night and day take place concurrently. Isaiah 40:22 Proverbs 8:27 Luke 17:34

Superstitious beliefs that earth is supported by four elephants or by the god (Atlas) or by a superhuman…etc., etc.,etc.	No superstitious ideas suggest earth's support system as other than God's creative process Job 26:7
Humans actually thought they could number the astronomical bodies all the way up to the year 1932 AD	Reveals the universe, space and planets as too large to be measured or counted. Genesis 15:5
Most beliefs identified humans as the first in the process of living creatures. Refuted now by scientific discovery.	Identifies the sequence of created living things from plants, water creatures, birds, mammals and humans. Genesis 1:11-28
Popular belief about lightening was that it was the gods throwing lighting bolts.	Teaches the natural process of weather storms and lightening Jeremiah 10:13 and 51:16
Believed that different cultures of humans are from different origins	Teaches that all humans are blood relatives Acts 17:26
Superstition of gods constantly pouring out water on the earth	Scientific water cycle Ecclesiastes. 1:7 Job 36:27, 28

What does this all say to us? It says that the writers of the Bible (although uneducated) had a scientific knowledge that far exceeded any human capacity of their time. These men were way ahead of any human discoveries, to reveal things that would not be scientifically proven for many centuries into the future.

Can anyone honestly consider the facts without coming to the realization that, the book we call the Bible is a miraculous revelation of superhuman origin? Anyone with a pure mind and scholarly concerns must accept the Divine origin of the Bible. There are no other alternatives.

THE BIBLE'S POPULARITY

Intelligent people read the Bible. By intelligent, I mean those who have an interest in knowing what life is really all about. Without a basic understanding of what the Bible teaches, a person is still ignorant on life's basic realities...no matter how much education he or she claims to possess.

The Bible is read by more people and published in more languages than any other book in history. Statistics from the British Foreign Bible Society reveal that, to meet demands for the Bible from the 1960's, they had to print one copy every three seconds around the clock (every 24 hours). That meant they had to print 22 copies of the Bible every minute, 1369 copies every hour...32,876 copies every day of the year. Think about that, and then multiply 32,876 x 365 days a year...every year.

WHAT ABOUT THE APOCRYPHA?

Jewish people acknowledge only the thirty-nine books of Hebrew Scriptures (Old Testament) as sacred scripture. Protestant Christians add another twenty-seven books (New Testament) to the Old Testament as their Bible (total 66 books). The Roman Catholic Church and the Eastern Orthodox Church acknowledge the Old Testament, the New Testament and the Apocrypha as part of sacred scripture (total 73 books).

12

Several books are included in the Apocrypha and are cataloged by some intellectuals as prophetic, historical, wisdom, and even romantic literature. The term "apocrypha" comes from a Greek word that means, "hidden" or "secret"…to suggest the writings grouped under this term as containing hidden truth that only certain people could discern and comprehend. In other words…only a deeply spiritual, pious and devout scholar would be qualified to translate the hidden tenets, precepts, ideologies and doctrinal realities contained in the Apocrypha.

In reality, the Apocrypha isn't all that special. While some of the writings do have limited historical value, to fill in the 400-year historical gap between the Old Testament and the New Testament…the theological and doctrinal teachings do not confirm with other Biblical truth. Although the Roman Catholic Church continues to declare them as part of their scripture, the Apocrypha is a highly debatable group of writings.

WHAT'S IN A NAME?

The word "Bible" does not appear anywhere in the Bible. The word came from a Greek term for an Egyptian plant (papyrus) used to make paper. The ancient Phoenician city (Byblos) took its name for its writing manufacturing industry. The Greeks used the term "biblos" for papyrus, and eventually, anything associated with writing (like scrolls) were also called "biblos".

Other popular terms associated with the Bible include "The Law and Prophets", "Holy Scriptures", "Word", "Word of God", and "The Truth of God".

Speaking of "God"...nowhere in the Bible is His name spelled correctly. After getting instructions from God to lead the children of Israel from Egypt, Moses wanted to know what to say about who sent him. God answered him this way; *"Tell them, "I AM" sent you"* (paraphrased).

Ancient Hebrew writings used only consonants, without vowels like the English (a, e, i, o, u). When they read out loud, they just added the vowel sounds. But when it came to the word "YHWH" (Hebrew for "I AM"), no vowel sounds were added and often another word was substituted. The Hebrews held deep respect for God's name (YHWH) and they were acutely fearful of profaning the use of His name. So, when the ancient Hebrew language died out, the ancient vowels used with the language were forgotten, including those used for YHWH.

Later, in the seventh century, a group of Jewish scholars known as the Masoretes, sought to preserve the ancient Hebrew language, adding vowels to the ancient writings. But when they came to YHWH they added vowels for the word "Lord", which is "Adonai" in the Hebrew language. English translators then later (from ignorance of the old Jewish tradition) combined the two words (Yhwh and Adonai). In doing so, they invented the word "Jehovah" ...which is not a correct spelling.

14

In other words, Jehovah is a word combining the consonants of one word and the vowels of another. The result is, no one in the world knows the true spelling for God's real name. I think God had it all planned that way.

JESUS' BIRTHDAY

Nope, Jesus wasn't born on Christmas, as a lot of people believe. There is no basis for defining December 25th as the birth of Christ. The Bible doesn't tell us when Jesus was born, even though it gives us the birthdays of Pharaoh and Herod. God probably planned it this way so that people would worship His Son rather than a day on the calendar. Still, it is a matter of curiosity of exactly when Jesus was born. We do know it wasn't in the winter months. Shepherds grazed and watched their flocks day and night for most of the year, but during the cold, rainy season they kept their flocks in shelters, not on a hillside. Logic suggests that Jesus was born in a good weather month.

What year was Jesus born? We're not totally sure, but we can come fairly close. Dionysius Exiguus (a sixth-century Roman Abbot) made a 4-5 year mistake in numbering the years of his new "Christian era". He sited the birth of Jesus at least four to five years later than what it actually was...which means, the birth of Christ is more likely to have occurred somewhere around 5 BC or 4 BC.

But, when you think about all this...and the way people now celebrate Christmas...it makes sense that God would keep the actual date of His Son a secret. It seems that everybody gets recognized with a gift except the One who really deserves it.

Same thing is true with Easter...a day that is supposed to represent the greatest event in the history of mankind (the resurrection of Christ). So, what do we do with it? We invented an Easter Bunny to replace Christ. Colored eggs are now more important than an empty tomb.

Ever wonder why Satan was so intent on inventing a Santa Claus and Easter Bunny? He doesn't want humans to get too excited about their eternal hope. He doesn't want us to focus on the two events that determine where we go after we die.

I wonder why there are no substitutes to distract people from the birth and death of other religious leaders or historical figures? Why did the devil just pick on Jesus? Why is there a Santa Claus and Bunny rabbit? Do you suppose Satan knows the reality and importance of Jesus' life and death? Think about it.

SUMMARY

We could go on and on about stuff in the Bible that most people aren't fully aware, but this should serve to satisfy our curiosity that "The Book" is more than just another book. From my years of private research I can honestly say with many other students...no other writing in the world compares with it. Everywhere we look, reality just keeps getting better and better.

The Bible's Origin
A True Miracle
That Goes Beyond Dispute

One of the miracles of the Bible is how it has all come together as a perfect book, to endure through the centuries as the most authoritative guide to our human existence. Even though it was written centuries ago, there are unlimited copies translated into every language throughout the world for everyone to read.

Some people are concerned that modern translations may distort the truths that God had intended for us to understand, but this is not an issue. The truths of God have been protected, as we will learn in this study. God has not only revealed His eternal truth to our human family...He has personally protected that truth throughout the ages, to assure that no truth would be lost.

I use the King James Version in my studies, realizing it has some confusing texts from the way the English language was spoken back in 1611 AD, when the King James was translated. Other people rely on other translations for their studies, which brings up the question..."Could two different people reading from two different translations come up with two differing interpretations of what the Bible says?" The answer (as far as the translations are concerned) is, no. But there are other factors involved in Bible interpretation, such as pre-conceived bias or philosophical opinions. More about this later in our study.

17

To help clarify the concern about where our Bible came from, and offer some assurance that God has protected His truth in all the translations, let's review the process of how the Bible finally came to us in modern print.

GOD'S FIRST COMMUNICATION WITH MANKIND WAS THROUGH THE SPOKEN WORD

The first communication that God had with mankind was oral (word of mouth) communication, since writing had not yet been invented. Beginning with Adam and Eve (first two humans) God communicated His message very intimately...by speaking directly (one-on-one) with them. Adam and Eve heard the certain voice of God as He walked with them on earth. They didn't read about God in a book.

Oral communication was God's method of relating to the first generations of our human family. The two sons of Adam and Eve (Cain and Abel) were also familiar with God's voice, and later in history God spoke directly to other people, such as Noah and Abraham, and with Abraham's sons (Isaac and Jacob).

As history progressed, God began to communicate to the masses of people through human prophets (preachers) who He personally selected to speak the words He placed upon their lips. These prophets told others only what God revealed to them...to assure that all people would know God's eternal message.

"God, who at sundry times and in divers manners spake in time past unto the fathers by the prophets, hath in these last days spoken unto us by his Son, whom he hath appointed heir of all things, by whom also he made the worlds". Hebrews 1:1

GOD'S SECOND COMMUNICATION WITH MANKIND WAS THROUGH THE WRITTEN WORD

Eventually, writing was invented...of which God took advantage to share His message with the human family. An early example was God's Ten Commandments written on tablets of stone and given to Moses for the children of Israel on.

" And the LORD said unto Moses, Come up to me into the mount, and be there: and I will give thee tables of stone, and a law, and commandments which I have written; that thou mayest teach them. "   Exodus 24:12

Other men later followed Moses...to speak and write the words of God as "they were moved (inspired) by the Holy Spirit" to record an accurate, infallible account of God's message.

"We have also a more sure word of prophecy; whereunto ye do well that ye take heed, as unto a light that shineth in a dark place...Knowing this first, that no prophecy of the scripture is of any private interpretation. For the prophecy came not in old time by the will of man: but holy men of God spake as they were moved by the Holy Ghost."   2 Peter 1:19-21

19

GOD'S THIRD COMMUNICATION
WITH MANKIND WAS THROUGH JESUS...
GOD'S ONLY BEGOTTEN SON

Finally, after centuries of communicating through Old Testament prophets, the time came for God's son (Jesus) to visit the earth. His life on earth revealed the perfect character of God and made the full will of God known to all mankind.

During his earthly visit Jesus assembled a small group of disciples (12)...to who he taught the deeper truths of God. These disciples were given the responsibility of taking and teaching the message of Jesus into all the world. This was the next phase of God's communication with the human race.

After Jesus' death and ascension back to heaven, these first disciples were very aggressive in obeying the command of Christ...to take His word throughout the then-known world, as personal witnesses to the person and ministry of Jesus. Because of their teaching, those disciples gave their lives as martyrs... which is a powerful confirmation that they believed and trusted the Jesus they preached. And because these twelve men were "inspired" of God, they made no mistakes in their teaching.

God spoke directly to these first disciples through the Holy Spirit, who guided them to teach and write the exact words God wanted them to record...making certain that there would be no errors in what they wrote. Our current Bible is a record of both the Old Testament prophets and New Testament disciples.

20

THE BIBLE'S MAKE UP

The Bible consists of sixty-six books. Thirty-nine books make up the Old Testament, which were all written centuries before the birth of Christ. Twenty-seven books make up the New Testament, which were written by the disciples of Jesus after His death and resurrection.

The Hebrew Old Testament that existed at the time when Jesus was on earth (from which he read and taught) is the same Old Testament that we have today (the same thirty-nine books).

The chapter and verse divisions in the Bible that make it convenient to reference, were made later in history by Stephen Langton (Archbishop of Canterbury, England) who divided the Bible into chapters. Robert Stephanus (a printer in Paris) further divided the Bible into verses.

The use of *italics* first appeared in the Geneva Bible to identify words that _were not_ in the original Hebrew and Greek manuscripts, but which had been added by the translators to complete an intended thought. But, while the intention of italicized words was to make a thought clearer...a translator could be in error to the original thought, which the italicized words helps to prevent. One example is the word "*unknown*" in reference to a gift of tongues. This word, which was not in the original text, was added later for text clarification. Unfortunately it has created some doctrinal confusion in some teachings.

21

A student, who might question a particular passage or word in his or her current Bible, can return to the original Greek and Hebrew manuscripts for a more precise rendition...although God's basic truths have been maintained in most modern-day translations. A person does not need to be a language scholar in order to understand God's basic truths.

The Old Testament

In the times of Jesus, every Jewish community had the part of the Bible known as the Old Testament. It was handwritten on scrolls and kept in the synagogue where people met for religious instruction and worship. The scrolls were rolls of goat or sheepskins from ten to thirty feet long. Most often, a scroll contained one whole book of the Bible.

The Old Testament deals primarily with the nation of Israel (the descendants of Abraham). Some of the books are historical while others are prophetical (to tell future events that would happen to Israel before the birth of Christ).

The Old Testament books were initially written in the Hebrew language but, by the time of Christ, the Old Testament had been translated into the Greek language, which was at that time an international language.

During his earthly ministry, Jesus read and taught from these Old Testament scrolls in the synagogue at Nazareth. In doing so, Jesus gave credibility to their authenticity.

The New Testament

The New Testament was written after the life, death and resurrection of Jesus. The first four books of the New Testament are known as the "Gospels", which means "good news". They are so called because they tell of the earthly life of Jesus, the Christ, who came to earth sharing God's good news of salvation.

The New Testament also shares some of the experiences of Jesus' early followers as they went forth teaching the good news of Christ as they were commanded to do. The zeal of their ministry reveals the importance of their message.

The New Testament also includes letters written by the apostle Paul and other apostles to the early Christian churches throughout the Mediterranean world. Copies of these letters were made and circulated for other neighboring churches to read... providing Christian instruction for the new converts. These letters, along with copies of the gospel writings, were widely circulated throughout the Roman Empire, even though the early Christians were exposed to Roman persecution for doing so.

THE ORIGINAL BIBLE WRITINGS
LATER TRANSLATED INTO MODERN LANGUAGES

In 410 AD a scholar by the name of Jerome worked 25 years to translate the entire Bible from the original Hebrew and Greek into everyday Latin (the common language of the people in the western world at that time).

Jerome's translation (known as the "Vulgate") is still the official text of the Roman Catholic Church. The word "Vulgate" means "common" or "ordinary", referring to the common use of it by the church. But by the eighth century, the only people who could understand the Latin language were the scholars...which prompted a monk known as the "Venerable Bede" to translate the Latin Vulgate Bible into Anglo-Saxon, the language that was then being spoken in England.

Later, in the fourteenth century, John Wyclif and cohorts completed the first English translation of the entire Bible...but authorities within the Roman Catholic church did all they could to destroy Wyclif's translation. This prompted additional copies to be written secretly by hand, parts of which Wyclif distributed to his followers (called Lollards).

The Lollards zealously traveled all over England reading this translation to the people...but many who read or listened to Wyclif's version were punished (even burned at the stake) by order of the Catholic Church. Wyclif, however, died in 1384 AD before he could be punished.

The Wyclif Bible survived despite persecution, and was widely used throughout the 15th century. Many people, who were so hungry for spiritual truth, paid the equivalent of more than 200 dollars for a complete Wyclif Bible, while others gave a load of hay for a few chapters from one single translated book.

24

In the sixteenth century, Martin Luther (a Roman Catholic priest) began to affirm the Bible's supremacy. He challenged the Catholic Church and the German government by declaring that only the Word of God governed his conscience.

Motivated by his desire to make the Bible understood by all people, Luther prepared a German translation using dramatic everyday expressions to help the average reader. His translation was not based on the Latin Vulgate used by the Catholic Church but more closely on the original Hebrew and Greek manuscripts. Luther's convictions and efforts had considerable influence on other English translations that followed. Even today, some Protestants in Germany still use the Luther Bible.

But, while Luther's work was important, it was William Tyndale who became the most influential 16th century English Bible translator. Tyndale believed that all people had a right to know the scriptural promises made to them, and that they should not be expected to read Latin just to read the Bible. He knew that only a new translation in the English language could meet the people's hunger for the scriptures.

Johann Gutenberg (inventor of movable type) produced the first printed Bible in the Latin language. Later, Tyndale's New Testament was the first to be printed in English... but it had to be printed in Germany, because the King of England and the Catholic Church prohibited the people's use of Tyndale's Bible.

Copies of Tyndale's New Testament (printed in the English language) were smuggled from Germany into England in shipments of grain and cloth. But while working on an English translation of the Old Testament, Tyndale was betrayed, arrested and condemned to be strangled and burned. His last words were a prayer, "Lord, open thou the King of England's eyes."

Tyndale's translations were written in a simple form of English that characterized the simple language of the people. His New Testament was based from Erasmus' Greek and Latin texts; the Latin Vulgate; and Luther's German New Testament. His Old Testament translation was based mainly from the original Hebrew...but Tyndale died before completing it, leaving the job to Miles Coverdale to complete. Tyndale's complete Bible was printed and dedicated to Henry VIII, who authorized it in 1537 after a new edition was printed in England.

The notes and prefaces in the Tyndale and Coverdale joint translation created so many disputes that Henry VIII authorized another Bible that included no controversial material. The new Bible was known as the Great Bible because of its great size. Copies had to be chained in the churches for safekeeping, as people swarmed to hear it read. But when Mary Tudor (a Roman Catholic) came to the throne, she outlawed the public use of the Great Bible. This set off an underground effort to make the Bible accessible for common readers.

26

Scholars fled from England to Geneva, Switzerland... where they produced a new version of the Bible after much study of the Greek and Hebrew manuscripts. The Geneva Bible was published as a small book that could be used by ordinary people. It quickly became the most popular version.

Later (1604), England's King James called a conference to consider serious differences of opinion over versions of the Bible then in existence. At that conference a new translation was suggested that would have approval of the whole church. A commission of 54 scholars was appointed to undertake this new revision, basing their work on a study of early Hebrew and Greek manuscripts, as well as many of the later translations. The new Bible (King James Version) immediately replaced all the other versions being used in the churches. During the next fifty years, it became the most popular version for use in the home.

The King James Version was the result of three years of concentrated effort by fifty-four scholars, after which an extra nine months was needed for final editing. No marginal notes were inserted, except to explain some Greek and Hebrew words. As a result, it was not as controversial as previous versions.

When the United States became a nation, Bibles still had to be imported from England and Holland. It was Robert Aitken who printed the first English Bible in America. It was an edition of the King James Version.

This first printing was commended to the public by a special U.S. Congressional resolution. Our country's forefathers valued the Holy Scriptures so highly that in 1816 they founded the American Bible Society to translate and publish the Holy Scriptures, and to encourage its circulation. The first president of ABS was Elias Boudinot, who was president of the Continental Congress and friend of George Washington.

As scholarly investigation advanced, new versions of the Bible have emerged to help improve upon earlier versions. More original manuscripts have been discovered and the older ones are better understood. Archeological discoveries have also helped to illuminate certain portions of scripture.

As knowledge of ancient manuscripts continues to grow, along with new Archaeological discoveries and changes in the English language itself, it becomes more apparent that additional translations are needed to keep up with the pace. But while these new revisions alter the language...they do not change the history, or truth, which the Bible shares with us. You and I can be assured that the original truths from God are perfectly preserved and transmitted to us in these latter days.

God promised, *"Heaven and earth shall pass away, but my words shall not pass away."* History and science have confirmed this promise to be valid. The truth of God's word has remained intact throughout the centuries.

MANUSCRIPT INTEGRITY

New Testament

There are more than 24,000 partial and complete ancient manuscript copies of the New Testament. Added to that number are better than 86,000 quotations from the early church fathers, as well as several thousand Lectionaries that contain Scripture quotations from the early centuries of Christianity. What this means is...there is an awesome amount of evidence in support of the New Testament credibility.

Critics hasten to point out New Testament "manuscript variants", numbering somewhere around 150,000, to suggest a compromising breakdown of Bible integrity. For those ignorant of the facts, this may appear to be a staggering indictment, but the truth is...it's no where near as bad as it sounds.

Ninety-nine percent of these "variants" have no urgent importance or influence on truth. Most involve a missing letter in a word or a reversal of two words (such as Christ Jesus rather than Jesus Christ). Only about 50 of the variants have any real significance...but even those offer no threat of misinterpreting any of God's moral commandments or doctrinal truth.

The Bible, which has been passed down to us in modern translations, can be accepted as God's perfect word...to reveal to us God's perfect will for our life. It still contains the truth of the original, just as God revealed it to His prophets and disciples.

29

In comparison to other ancient books, the Bible stands alone in its manuscript reliability and authenticity. No secular classic from antiquity can claim more accurate or earlier dating manuscript copies than those we have of the Bible. Research scholars continually confirm how remarkably intact the New Testament texts are in comparison to other writings.

While ancient secular works have only a few manuscript copies on which to depend, the New Testament has thousands of manuscripts as a basis for authority. And while the average gap between an original secular writing and its earliest copy is over 1,000 years...the New Testament copies show up in a few years.

What all this means is...the New Testament has a far greater basis of credibility than all other writings of antiquity, as it has an abundance of early records for comparison, to assure us that a proper transmission of the original writings has transpired.

Additional confirmations, beyond manuscript integrity, include an enormous number of testimonies from early church leaders and worship books (written within 150-200 years from the time of Christ) that exceed well over 86,000...enough to recreate all but eleven verses of the entire New Testament.

As for the Old Testament, the Dead Sea Scrolls put to rest any doubt of its translated accuracy. Discovered at Qumran in 1947 AD, they contain O.T. manuscripts dating more than one thousand years earlier than those then in our possession.

The significance of that discovery is that, when the two manuscripts (Dead Sea and earlier) are compared, they both are basically identical. To scholarly researchers, the fact that these two manuscripts (separated by 1000 years) are so parallel is an amazing testament and proof of the precision and accuracy of Old Testament manuscript transmission.

For example, the two copies of the book of Isaiah that were discovered in a Qumran cave near the Dead Sea (1947 AD) are more than one thousand years earlier than the oldest dated manuscript previously known...yet they are identical (word for word) with our Hebrew Bible in more than ninety-five percent of the text. The five percent difference consists only in obvious slips of the pen and variations of spelling...not in the message content. Simply amazing!

The Dead Sea Scrolls are a convincing proof that the transcribers of Biblical manuscripts took great care in their work ...deeply aware that they were duplicating God's word. Those who copied the Bible's manuscripts went to phenomenal lengths to avoid any error from entering their transcription. The scribe was very vigilant to count every word, syllable, letter and line of both the original and their copy, to ensure total accuracy in their transcript. It is truly amazing how pure and accurate the copies of the Old and New Testaments have come down to us through the generations. Today's Bible is God's initial message.

Not only has a omniscient, omnipotent God spoken to our human family through His written word...He has also made certain to preserve His word for all generations.

No other writing in human history has been preserved with such great care as the Bible. No other writing in human history has as many transmitted manuscripts to confirm their message, as does the Bible. No other writing in human history is more accurate to the original as the Bible. No other writing in human history is the inspired written word of God.

Everywhere we look, reality just keeps getting better and better!

The Bible's Credibility
Amazing Facts That Confirm
The Undeniable Truth

Millions of books have been written about the Bible over many centuries. The researchers use words like miraculous, phenomenal, awesome and astounding to describe the book that has been read by more people than any other book in history. I'll just include the word, amazing…for that's the only conclusion a person can come away with, once they really dig into the facts of what the Bible is all about. Amazing!

What you are about to read in these next few pages is but a brief summary of the evidence that substantiates the Bible to be what it claims to be (the only true written word of God to the human race). No other writing, religious or otherwise, can make such a claim with any authority or credibility. The Bible stands alone and above any piece of literature ever produced.

Academic research demands three things as evidence for Biblical validity…

1. Proof that we have an exact record of the original writings of what God said and did

2. That the Bible is absolutely accurate in its historical record of people, places and events

3. That the Bible is "scientifically" sound, i.e. that it does not contain myths or scientific absurdity

33

THE SOLEMN REALITY

The Bible is a book that cannot be avoided. Only the most foolish person would reject the Bible as a source to guide them in life, without doing a personal, in-depth, investigation of where it came from and what it teaches. It's almost unbelievable that there are people who have never read the most popular book in the world. There are only three possibilities for what this book we call the Bible actually is...

1.   The Bible is an elaborate fraud conceived by a group of human beings to deceive the entire human race.

2.   The Bible is a collection of writings by confused and neurotic zealots attempting to exalt a mythical God.

3.   The Bible is the word of God as it claims, and is a Divine message from the Creator of the universe.

If the Bible is a fraud, then its teachings are lies and its prophecies are false predictions conceived by evil men...all of which could easily be identified and disproved.

If the Bible is a product of religious zealots who seek to promote a myth, then their teachings would not withstand the empirical scrutiny of scientists, historians and scholars.

But if the Bible is God's exact word, recorded by human scribes, then all of its teachings are truth and all its prophecies are accurate in precise detail. And, if the Bible is true, then none of its claims can be disproved.

THE AMAZING REALITY

The Bible has fulfilled all requirements to validate itself as a book of supernatural origin. Everything it says is supported by history, science and human experience. No sincere researcher can challenge the massive amount of irrefutable evidence in total support of the Bible's legitimacy as God's word.

It would take a library of books to discuss all the data confirming the Bible's legitimacy, so we will just review some of the highlights in this study. Every conceivable circumstance in life is in full harmony with the Bible.

Science, history, current events, fulfilled prophecy and human experiences all make powerful declarations that the Bible is a special work, far exceeding the wisdom and insight of all other knowledge. No other writing in the entire world, religious or otherwise, compares with the Bible's timeless and relevant message. And even though it has been translated into modern languages from the original manuscripts, the truth of the Bible is still intact. We still have God's original guidelines for our life.

The only conclusion for such wisdom and endurance is that the Bible is the word of an omniscient God...who not only inspired its writing, but has also protected it for every generation.

Eternal wisdom is available for those who desire to seek it. If you're looking for a truly amazing miracle...consider the Bible! It's a book that cannot be explained any other way.

EVIDENCE THAT THE BIBLE
IS AN EXACT RECORD
OF WHAT GOD SAID AND DID

The Bible's Origin...

Simply stated, the Bible is God's written revelation for the entire human race. It is the only book in which God reveals Himself and His will to our human family.

God's method in producing His written word is quite unique and extraordinary. God didn't write scrolls in the sky or imprint messages on the moon for us to read. He wrote a book. And God didn't call some guy into a cave to give him mystic visions for the human race. God chose a bunch of guys who were "inspired" of God to write exactly what He wanted them to write. God wrote "His Book" using human minds and hands.

The Bible is a collection of 66 different books that were recorded by 40 different human writers (scribes) over a period of some 1600 years. Each of these scribes recorded only the words given to them by the one true God. In other words, the 40 human writers recorded only those words that *God inspired* them to write...not words that they dreamed up in their own head.

> "All scripture is given by inspiration of God, and is profitable for doctrine, for reproof, for correction, for instruction in righteousness: that the man of God may be perfect, thoroughly furnished unto all good works." 2 Timothy 3:16-17

36

This raises the eyebrows of skeptics, who see the "inspiration" argument as a convenient way for Bible believers to explain away the Bible's 40 different "human writers". But the supernatural wisdom and unity of what these human scribes have recorded puts that skepticism to silence. No mere human beings could have written the Bible without inspiration from an omniscient (all-knowing) God. Consider this...

The scribes who recorded God's word were from every walk of life (kings, peasants, fishermen, statesmen, philosophers, poets, scholars, etc). Moses, who was the scribe of the Bible's first five books, was a political leader who was trained in Egypt. Paul, the most prolific scribe of the New Testament, was a Rabbi. Then there was Peter (a fisherman), Matthew (a tax collector), Luke (a physician), Solomon (a king), Nehemiah (a king's servant), Amos (a herdsman), Joshua (a military general) and Daniel (a prime minister)...all of who were chosen of God as scribes at different times in history to record God's word.

Every one of these scribes wrote the same message in perfect continuity with all the rest of the scribes, even though they had no opportunity to corroborate with one another about what to write. And, what about this...these "ordinary human beings" recorded events that would occur hundreds and thousands of years into the future with perfect 100% accuracy! Amazing! It's evident that "Somebody" bigger was behind it all.

God picked out three continents from where His word would be recorded (Asia, Africa, Europe) with His scribes in every conceivable situation (wildernesses, prisons, palaces, dungeons, a deserted island). Yet, these guys have recorded the most amazing and precise truths known to mankind. And they did it in three different languages...Hebrew (language of Judah), Aramaic (language of the Near East until the time of Alexander the Great) and Greek (international language at time of Christ).

With all that diverse background of place, situation and language, here's something really amazing...the Bible sitting on your table is a complete and congruent message in perfect detail ...no contradictions, no errors, no superstitious myths...just good old solid truth. Nothing is left out for us to wonder about. It's all there...wisdom from a bunch of guys who lived at different times, in different places, speaking different languages.

Thirty-nine of the sixty-six books are referred to as the Old Testament while twenty-seven books are known as the New Testament. These two testaments (covenants) are records of the two covenants that God has made with the human race.

The Old Testament was written in the Hebrew language centuries before the birth and life of Christ. It contains events and prophecies long before He was born. The New Testament was written in the Greek language after Jesus had lived on earth. It records the events of Jesus' life as well as His teachings.

Our current English Bibles have been translated from these two original languages (Hebrew and Greek)...and yes, the translations have accurately protected the original teachings. The original copies of the Hebrew and Greek manuscripts are still available for research and, although Bible scholars refer to them for more clarification in their studies, it is not necessary that the common reader of the Bible become a language expert in order to understand God's will and guidance for his or her life.

Here's something to chew around on...there are more than 24,000 ancient manuscript copies in existence of the New Testament alone, including 5,300 Greek manuscripts and well over 19,000 Latin Vulgate and other early editions. Compare that to other ancient writings, such as Homer's Iliad with only 643 surviving copies; Caesar's Gallic Wars (10 copies); Plato (7 copies); Aristotle (49 copies) and Herodotus' History (8 copies). The numbers tell the story of how perfectly preserved and certain we are of God's original truth.

Then there's this time thing...the time between original writings and their earliest copies. Take, for example, the writing of Aristotle (which some people swear by as a profound wisdom for their life). It took 1,400 years for somebody to make a copy. Then there's Plato's wisdom that took 1,200 years for the first copy to surface, while Caesar and Herodotus' stuff only took 1,000 and 1,300 years for copies to show up on the newsstand.

By comparison, copies of the original New Testament were recorded within a mere 25 years. But, if that still sounds too long between an original and first copy, let us be reminded that "oral memorization" was the science of study and teaching at that time in history. Mass printing was not yet invented, so memorization was the science of scholar and student. People did not rely on "written" materials for their knowledge, but rather on memory skills and oral communication. This is a tough concept to grasp in this electronics era, where a push of a button clicks us onto any topic we want to research. We no longer need memory, we now have computers to do that for us.

What all this is saying to us is this…the Bible is the most aggressive and reliable of all ancient writings in conveying its original teachings of its Author. The Bible does not depend on one guy's "cave experience" that was passed along by his good buddies and recorded several hundred years later. The Bible is not a collection of "religious myths" from an "enlightened" guru, priest, maharishi or great thinker. It is a collection of congruent truths that are beyond the mere wisdom and philosophies of men.

The origin and preservation of the Bible are powerful confirmations to its authenticity as God's word. When we think of the subtle and violent attacks to destroy the Bible and its truth throughout history, it is truly amazing that there remains a copy anywhere…but, then, its Author wants it to be read.

Had human beings been the architects of the Bible as its author, compiler and distributor...the result would have been a confused conglomeration of superstition and myth without any historical, scientific or rational logic (like all the other religious scriptures throughout the world). But the Bible is much different than those writings of human innovation.

Throughout its pages the Bible claims to be Divinely given...a claim made by no other book. The scribes of the Bible make statements such as "the word of the Lord came to me"; "God said"; "thus saith the Lord". By these statements the writers confess that they are mere scribes recording only what God had revealed to them. They were not the authors...only the scribes.

The Bible is not dependent, however, on just the claims of its scribes. The proof of being God's infallible and inspired word is also supported by the unity and perfect harmony of the Bible's message. Consider this...the 40 writers of the Bible, who lived over a period of 1600 years without any opportunity to corroborate with each other about what they were to write, all wrote the same exact message in perfect harmony and unity with one another.

This perfect harmony and unity of message is a strong statement that a Divine mind must be behind what these human writers recorded ... for how could 40 different men living in different generations have put together such a perfect book?

The Bible's Message...

We have already touched on the harmony and continuity of the Bible's message, but the uniqueness of its teaching takes the Bible one step further in defining it as an "amazing" book. Throughout its pages we are introduced to the supernatural, which we must either accept as truth or reject as fiction. The characters and events of the Bible are either an elaborate hoax to deceive the human family, or they are the words of a divine Creator who has revealed things that we would never have known otherwise.

Science has accepted the reality that no hoax exists, while some modern philosophers aren't so sure. Take miracles for example...the Bible is full of them. But, to some thinkers, miracles just don't happen. Their logic is that we live in a closed, functioning universe where everything operates within the rigid laws of nature...where miracles are not possible. Such thinking justifies all past, current and future events to have some natural explanation. The problem is, no one can explain it all.

The basis for belief in miracles is to believe in the reality of God. If we accept God, then we can accept miracles...as God has no limits to hinder His capacity to overrule nature. This is evident in the many miracles described in the Bible, including those performed in the life of Jesus Christ (God on earth). Would Jesus' followers all died as martyrs without seeing his miracles?

The Bible reveals events that we humans have never witnessed or that science cannot explain. For example, the report of creation is a simple and adequate account as to the beginning of all things. It tells from where the universe and earth began, as well as the origin of vegetable life; our atmosphere; the waters; the years, months and seasons; animal life; human life; sin; evil; death; the different races, nations and languages of people.

No legitimate scientific alternative has been produced to discredit the Biblical account of creation...or any other truth revealed in the scriptures for that matter. Although false science, human philosophy and cultish religions have tried, there is no adequate alternative to the origin of things beyond what the Bible teaches. True science and the Bible are not adversaries.

But the Bible was not written as a book of science. Its teachings are much more elevated...to reach into the meaning and purpose of life itself. It is the sole authority on matters of importance to human life and eternal existence.

The Bible provides sensible advice on moral, social, family, psychological and physical health issues...as well as the spiritual issue of relating to our Creator. In all the important matters involving our health and wellbeing, the Bible is superior in its wisdom. But, while the Bible is beneficial in its advice on the important issues we deal with in this life, its top priority reaches far beyond the few years we have on this earth.

The central message of the Bible is God's revelation of Himself and His will for our human family. It is a message with an invitation to every person on earth...an invitation to enjoy a relationship with our Creator. For this reason, an understanding of Biblical truth is the single most essential undertaking in our human education. Knowing what the Bible teaches will resolve life's fundamental issues that haunt and confuse many people.

We will look at the seven Bible stories in a later chapter that puts this all into perspective...but first, let's look at some of the criticisms that challenge the Bible's credibility.

Challenging Criticisms Of The Bible...

Some people argue that the Bible cannot be trusted, as it is full of contradictions, but that argument is grounded more on overreaction and ignorance rather than on the facts. One example is the <u>two</u> blind men at Jericho who came to Jesus for healing ... or was it only <u>one</u> blind man? Matthew's gospel tells us that there were <u>two</u> blind men but Mark and Luke refer only to <u>one</u>. So, what's the problem?

I have three daughters. Suppose all three came to my house at different times one day...and I told the wife that Midge stopped by. The next day I told her that Pam and Anna came by the house. Did I contradict myself? Think about it. Just because I mentioned only <u>one</u> of the girls didn't mean I was technically incorrect in my conversation. Bad example to disprove the Bible!

44

Other criticisms include things like, "Did the men hear a voice at Paul's conversion or didn't they?"... "Was the sun created first or was the light?" ... "How could a whale with a small mouth swallow a man (Jonah)?" ... "If Jesus was crucified on Friday and rose on Sunday, how could he have been in the grave for three days and three nights?" ... "Did Judas hang himself or did he die by falling headlong and bursting open?"

These are a few examples from critics who frantically try to find something wrong with the Bible. Some criticisms arise from false language interpretations. Some come from ignorance of history and cultural customs. Other criticisms are caused by unfamiliarity with conditions on which commands were given, and some are simply the result of dull spiritual perception (dealing with the finite while the Bible deals with the infinite).

We could spend a month of Sundays answering these and other objections, but that isn't the purpose of this writing. Let me just say this...every alleged contradiction supposedly in the Bible has been satisfactorily resolved.

Still need more proof before we move on? How about this...the mouth and throat of a whale is too small to devour a human...but the Bible never said that a whale swallowed Jonah.

"Now the Lord had prepared a great fish to swallow up Jonah. And Jonah was in the belly of the fish three days and three nights."   Jonah 1:17

If I read that scripture right, God created a big fish (not a whale) with a mouth big enough to swallow Jonah. Wonder who came up with the idea that it was a "whale"? For all I know, it could have been a wide-mouthed bass with a very large tummy that God made just for this one occasion.

The point in all this is...the Bible has survived all its critics who suggest it to be full of contradictory statements. You and I have this assurance...that the message of the Bible has been proven without doubt. What it says is what has happened... which brings us to another powerful evidence of its Divine authorship.

The Bible's Amazing Prophetical Ability...

The Bible is the only book in all of history that has been proven through every test of critical empirical scrutiny as the genuine word of God to His creation. One of the most powerful witnesses to the Bible's divine authorship is its ability to predict future events with perfect 100% precision. No mere human being has such ability, defining the Bible as unique and God authored.

Feeble attempts have tried to discredit Bible prophecies by suggesting them to be post-dated, i.e....that they were written after the event. Those arguments have been quieted by scientific and historical evidence. Historical scholars know, beyond doubt, that all Bible prophecies were recorded long before the event occurred, even as early as several centuries prior to the event.

It is known that the Old Testament was translated into the Greek language (Septuagint) about 280 BC, which means that all the prophecies in the Old Testament were recorded prior to that date. It is further known that the four Gospel books of the New Testament were recorded prior to the year 24 AD. All prophesied historical events that occurred after 280 BC and 24 AD must be accepted as fulfillment of prophecy.

In another writing titled "The Final Days Of Mankind", we look at Bible prophecies in much detail, but for this study we will only take a brief tour.

OLD TESTAMENT PROPHESIES

The Israelite (Jewish) People...

Most Old Testament prophecy deals with the Jewish people (Hebrew, Israelite) who trace their lineage back to a man named Abraham, who lived about 4,000 years ago. Abraham had a deep faith in God and, as a result, was greatly blessed of God ...receiving from God these promises...

"Now the LORD had said unto Abraham, Get thee out of thy country, and from thy kindred, and from thy father's house, unto a land that I will show thee: And I will make of thee a great nation, and I will bless thee, and make thy name great; and thou shalt be a blessing: And I will bless them that bless thee, and curse him that curseth thee: and in thee shall all families of the earth be blessed." Genesis 12:1-3

47

"And the LORD said unto Abram, after that Lot was separated from him, Lift up now thine eyes, and look from the place where thou art northward, and southward, and eastward, and westward: For all the land which thou seest, to thee will I give it, and to thy seed for ever. And I will make thy seed as the dust of the earth: so that if a man can number the dust of the earth, then shall thy seed also be numbered."   Genesis 13

God made four distinct promises to Abraham...

1. Abraham would be the father of a great nation
2. Abraham would have a great (respected) name
3. Through Abraham all other nations would be blessed
4. A land forever belonging to Abraham's descendents

Several hundred years after God's promises, there are millions of Abraham's descendents heading to their promised land under the leadership of Moses...just as God had promised. These descendents (known as Jews, Hebrews, Israelites) would soon enter the country that God had reserved for them, to set up their Jewish nation after 400 years of slavery in Egypt.

But before they were allowed to enter the promised land, God had some instructions and warnings for the Jews, to assure their national and political autonomy. God warned them that any disobedience to His laws would result in the removal of His protection...which would destabilize and threaten their national security (Deuteronomy chapters 28-33).

God was able to see into the future, to know that these descendents of Abraham would not heed His instructions and warnings. As a result, they would be deposed by other nations and scattered throughout the whole earth as strangers in unfamiliar countries. Even so, God promised that He would bring them back into their land...a promise that has held true.

Sadly, the descendents of Abraham did not listen to God's warning and fell into idolatry. As a result, they were overthrown and removed from their homeland, and scattered throughout the world. One aggressor after another toppled the Israelite nation in fulfillment of God's warning.

King Nebuchadnezzar of Babylon was the first to depose the Jews. In 606 BC he took the Jews captive to Babylon and then, in 586 BC, he burned the city of Jerusalem along with the Jewish temple. Later in history (70 AD) the Jews were again defeated when Titus' army destroyed Jerusalem and scattered the Israelites. As a result of the Roman incursion, the Jews wandered all over the world for 1900 years as persecuted strangers in other countries...leading up to their most painful persecution during the Nazi holocaust of World War II (1937-1945 AD).

But even in all the tragedies that should have consumed them, Abraham's descendents did not lose their identity. The state of Israel was restored in 1948 AD, after which time the scattered Jewish people have been returning to their homeland.

In 1967 AD, as a result of the miraculous six-day war, the Jewish people recaptured their capital city, Jerusalem, to regain full control for the first time in 2500 years.

Conversely, all the nations who opposed and persecuted Abraham's descendents, no longer exist. They have long ago faded into history while Abraham's descendents have survived, just as the God of Abraham promised many centuries previous. Apparently, God's promises do not fail.

One promise God made to Abraham, however, is often overlooked. It reads… *"In you all the families of the earth shall be blessed"*. This was both a promise and a prophesy of the coming Messiah…who would be born from Jewish lineage as a direct descendent of Abraham. The Messiah (Christ) would "bless all nations", as He was to come to earth to reveal God and to be a living sacrifice…so that all people of every nation could be restored to the fellowship of their Creator.

The historical Jesus who we read about in the Bible has fulfilled all the Old Testament Messianic prophecies in precise detail, to confirm Jesus as the true Christ that God promised to the world. The historical reality of Jesus, and the vast number of prophecies spoken of him prior to his birth, is evidence to his authority…and to the Bible's credibility.

It is nothing short of amazing that the Bible has the capacity to see the future with such perfect precision.

The Gentile Nations…

In another writing we look at some Old Testament prophecies regarding Gentile nations…prophecies with a much different outcome than that of Israel. We will not take the space here to repeat that study, other than to say how remarkable it is to researchers that the Bible has so much authority in looking into the future…to describe the harsh outcome of nations, cities and people who violated the authority of the one true God.

Gentile (non-Jewish) nations constantly rebelled against God's authority…only to reap the tragic harvest of that rebellion. In His mercy, God sent prophets to warn these people of the sure judgment that was to come…but they rejected God's overtures. The results are history. The former majesty of once powerful Gentile nations is now reduced to piles of dirt and rubble, with only a historical interest to archaeological research.

The ancient city, Tyre, is one example of God's warning and wrath on the rebellion and idolatry of the Gentiles. Tyre was inhabited with an arrogant, rebellious people who continually provoked the God of creation…to bring down His judgment on their city. The prophet, Ezekiel, revealed Tyre's future fate as total defeat and ruin via its enemies, never again to be rebuilt. History confirms the prophetical accuracy to the minutest of detail. A bare rock where the once proud city formerly stood is a powerful reminder of God's judgment and prophetical skill.

51

Another example is the city, Sidon, which also lodged a rebellious, arrogant people. God's pronounced judgment through His prophet, Ezekiel, declared their future fate to be a city of war, pestilence and blood. Just as Ezekiel prophesied, Sidon has one of the bloodiest histories on record. Throughout its history Sidon has seen blood flow in her streets by aggressors from every side, yet it would not become extinct like its sister-city, Tyre. Only God could have known these two different outcomes.

Two other Philistine cities (Gaza and Ashkelon) also suffered God's wrath as a result of rebellion. God's prophets (Amos, Jeremiah, Zephaniah) defined three distinct fates. One, the Philistines would no longer exist. Two, Gaza would become "bald". Three, Ashkelon would be destroyed, but would revive as a city for Judah's remnants to re-inhabit. History confirms the precise fulfillment of these three prophecies. The Philistines have been cut off from the earth, so completely, that not one Philistine is living anywhere in the world today. Ashkelon was totally destroyed but, after many centuries of lying in desolate waste, has been revived and is now a thriving community. Only God could have known the different outcomes.

Another group of Gentiles (the Edomites) were told their fate from six of God's prophets (Isaiah, Jeremiah, Ezekiel, Joel, Amos, Obadiah). It would be a violent and bloody history. Their land would be deserted where only wild animals would inhabit.

Again, God's prophecies proved to be 100% accurate. The Nabeans, Jews and Romans all had a hand in Edom's destruction, attacking at different times. Just before the Roman siege on Jerusalem in 70 AD, there were some 20,000 Edomites admitted to Jerusalem. These Edomites repaid their hosts with robbery and bloodshed. Then, as the Romans approached to attack the city, the Edomites fled Jerusalem rather than fight as allies with the Jews.

From that time in history, the Edomites as a distinct people, disappeared from the pages of history. Only traces of former glory are evident in the ruins of Archaeological digs. Petra, once capital to the land of Edom, was one of the true wonders of the ancient world. Built on a solid rock with its buildings hewn from solid rose-red rock, Petra was an awesome sight to behold. Today, the glory is gone. The ruins are inhabited with eagles, hawks, owls, lizards, vipers, serpents, scorpions, lions, leopards and wild goats...rather than by human beings, who stay away for fear of the animal and insect population.

Edom is now a desolate, unpopulated country resulting from many years of bloody battles that have left it suitable only for wild animals to roam. That such a thing could happen to Edom is totally amazing to scholars and historians...yet, this is precisely the prophecy of God way back 2500 years ago. Edom is just another reminder of the Bible's total credibility.

Then there's Moab and Ammon, the two sovereignties once located east of the Dead Sea, whose fate was prophesied by Ezekiel and Jeremiah...

1. Easterners would capture the land to live off the fruits
2. Men of the East would build palaces on Ammon

Jeremiah's prophecy about Ammon becoming desolate seemed unlikely, if not impossible, taking into account Ammon's enormous wealth and power at the time of his prophecy. Yet, that's exactly what happened. God's prophet spoke correctly and decisively, to reveal the future humiliation of a once proud and wealthy providence. And, even more remarkable, is the fact that Emir Abdullah (eastern ruler of Trans-Jordania) built his palace there...just as predicted. Today, the city of Ammon has about 20,000 inhabitants, some of which are officials of other nations. This amazing prophecy of Jeremiah (2500 years ago) that has been perfectly and precisely fulfilled, is one more example of the total credibility of the Bible.

Ezekiel's prophecies deal with several Egyptian cities, two of which are Thebes and Memphis.

1. The idols of Memphis would be destroyed
2. There would no more be an Egyptian prince
3. Thebes would be destroyed and fired
4. The multitudes would be cut off from Thebes

The ancient city "Noph" (later known as Memphis) was highly revered by Egyptians as the city where temple services began in worship of the gods. Idols were viewed with such deep respect in early Memphis history that opposing armies used them as tactics in fighting against and defeating the Egyptians.

Memphis survived (at least for a while) to exist second only to Alexandria in area. But the founding of Cairo (another nearby Egyptian city) lured much of the dwellers and objects away from Memphis, to relocate in Cairo. This resulted in Memphis' decline around the seventh century AD.

Historians are surprised that there is so little left of the once-grand ancient city. The scattered and meager relics left on the spot where Memphis once stood is a witness to God's judgment against idolatry...as well as giving support to the Bible's remarkable prophetical ability.

A neighboring city (Thebes) also suffered God's swift and decisive judgment. Two destructive blows came upon the rebellious and idolatrous city to mark its destruction. The first came at the hands of Cambyses, whose attack on Thebes was unusually destructive...as his armies destroyed the gigantic idol statues while ravaging and burning the idol worship temples.

A second attack rendered Thebes even more helpless, and then around 89 BC, a three-year siege tore down the city, sending it into historical oblivion, never again to rebound.

Ezekiel prophesied that the idols of Memphis' would be destroyed and that Thebes would be broken up…never again to be a prosperous and influential metropolis. Massive numbers of people, who once lived within its walls, never returned. Once a religiously significant city of wealth and craftsmanship, Thebes was divided into small villages that exist to modern times. History has confirmed that God's prophet was able to see the future with perfect clarity.

Another remarkable Old Testament prophecy against the idolatrous Gentile people was that of God's prophet, Nahum, against Nineveh. It is an amazing prophecy when we consider how powerful and fortified the city was against any potential military aggression. The same was also true of Babylon …but as history reveals, God's prophets saw beyond the iron grips of human effort, to reveal the judgments of God.

Nineveh was the proud and evil capital of the Assyrian Empire. God, in His mercy, sent Nahum to the city to reveal their evil and invite them to repent…but Nineveh did not heed the message, nor did they repent of their evils. God, then, sent Nahum to Nineveh with a prophetical warning…

1. Nineveh would be destroyed in a state of drunkenness
2. Nineveh would be destroyed in an overflowing flood
3. Nineveh would be burned
4. Nineveh would be totally destroyed (never rebuilt)

56

The defenses of Nineveh were elaborate and imposing. No other ancient city compared in size or strength. The city was seven miles in circumference, surrounded by a 150-foot wide moat. An inner wall, measuring 100 feet tall and 50 feet thick, with 200-foot tall towers, had been built to further fortify the city from foreign aggressors. An enemy would have to battle through 2200 feet (one-half mile) of deep ditches and walls to reach the inner city. Nineveh was an overwhelming (if not impossible) challenge. Yet the prophet, Nahum, declared its overthrow.

In less than 50 years after the prophet was sent to warn Nineveh of its evils...the greatly fortified city fell to its enemies. Today, where the once proud and evil Nineveh once stood, there remains only a mound of dirt that travelers walk over. God's prophecy was precisely fulfilled. Nineveh was destroyed by a flood and drunkenness; burned and destroyed, never to resurface.

The same decisive end that Nineveh suffered was also the fate of Babylon, another ancient city that now sits as a pile of dirt in testimony of God's judgment against evil. The once busy and famous city of great buildings occupied 196 square miles. It was a city to behold, but it was not to last, as revealed by the prophecies of Isaiah and Jeremiah.

The prophecies against Babylon are harsh and decisive. They define God's wrath against a people who trusted in their culture and learning, to become immorally decadent.

1.   Babylon would become like Sodom and Gomorrah, never again be inhabited

2.   Babylon's ruins will be infested by desert creatures and covered with swamps of water

Although the prophecy declared Babylon would become as Sodom and Gomorrah, this was not a prediction that Babylon would be destroyed in the same manner. It simply defined the end result...that these evil empires would not survive.

Where is ancient Babylon now? It's an uninhabited dirt pile and swamp. The former site of Babylon is a naked, repulsive wasteland where only desert wild beasts dwell (owls, jackals, etc.) and where the soil prohibits the growth of vegetation suitable for grazing animals, with no sheepfolds there. Arab superstitions prevent them from pitching their tents in the area and, though most ancient city sites attract tourists, Babylon has few visitors. This once powerful city has gone the way of all others who rejected and opposed the warnings of God.

Babylon was both a religious and commercial metropolis with great influence in its day. The evidence to its idolatry is revealed in the 53 temples to honor the chief gods; the 300 chapels to earthly gods; the 600 chapels for heavenly deities; the 180 altars for the goddess, Ishtar; the 180 altars for the gods Nergal and Adad; the 55 chapels to Marduk; and 12 other altars for various other gods. God's judgment was inevitable.

Samaria at one time had been Israel's northern capital...
but its people turned from God to worship idols...bringing God's
harsh judgment upon them. God's prophets (Hosea and Micah)
reveal just how strongly the wrath of God would come to this
backslidden people. The city would be violently overthrown to
become a heap in the field, its stone foundations poured down
into the valley. Samaria's once great splendor would be replaced
with planted vineyards...its idols reduced to memory. History
reveals just how accurate the prophecy was.

In 722 BC the sword of Sargon's army captured Samaria
with violent aggression. In 331 BC Alexander's army captured
Samaria with violent aggression. In 120 BC John Hyrcanus'
army captured Samaria with violent aggression. Each of these
armies caused great damage and death. The once imperial city of
the "ten tribes" of Israel (who revolted from the house of David)
is now transformed into gardens and vineyards. Observers define
Samaria as a pathetic village with a few neglected houses
occupied by plunderers. There are only a few pillar shafts left
standing as evidence of past glory. The streets are plowed up,
covered with olive gardens and cornfields.

While the glory of Samaria has long been destroyed, her
testimony of past sins survives as a pile of stones and rubbish
scattered on the slope of a hill. God's prophets told it right...just
as only an omniscient God could have predicted.

The ancient world housed many places for religious worship (Memphis, Thebes, Nineveh, Babylon and Jerusalem). Those places where man has tried to elevate pagan gods to an equal status with the one true God have long been destroyed, their ruins a reminder of God's supreme authority.

The only ancient city that is still among us is the one that has faithfully claimed the one and only Jehovah God. That city is Jerusalem, which should not have survived the horrendous assaults by its enemies. God, however, is bigger than all armies combined...and Jerusalem still exists as an announcement of God's protection for those who glorify His name.

All the prophecies of those ancient nations have been fulfilled precisely in every detail. There are more Old Testament prophecies regarding other ancient cities and peoples, but these should be sufficient to make the point. The mathematical probability of these prophecies being fulfilled as given is 1 in 5 x 10^9 (1 in 50,000,000,000). But history does not lie...confirming the Bible's remarkable ability to predict future events. The only conclusion is that God is behind it all.

This brings us to the central person of the Bible, our Creator...who has revealed Himself to our human family in three persons (Father, Son and Holy Spirit). As Jesus (the Son), God came to earth in human flesh to reveal Himself more intimately to our human family...but not without controversy.

The Life And Teachings Of Jesus...

The miraculous life of Jesus (God-Man) has been the theme of debate for many people. To some, the New Testament story is no more than a myth invented by zealous followers of a convicted troublemaker. To others, Jesus is the incarnate God who came to earth to reveal Himself and to offer sacrifice for our sinful rebellion.

This debate is crucial to the establishment of Biblical credibility. Was Jesus a hoax, a liar, a deceiver...or was he who he claimed to be? Did Jesus actually exist and, if so, how could he have been both God and man? Maybe Jesus was just a good man, a great prophet...but how can we accept him to be a God?

If the Bible is wrong in its declaration of Jesus, then everything else in the Bible is suspect as well. For this reason we will take the space in this study to briefly discuss the life and teachings of Jesus in order to establish credibility for what the Bible teaches.

There is no argument about how the Bible defines the historical person of Jesus. It is emphatic in declaring him to be "Immanuel" (God with us)...towering above all earthly heroes and the finest characters of fiction created by men. No human writer(s) could have invented such a person as Jesus Christ. Both the Old and New Testament writers describe the "human" Jesus of Nazareth with all the attributes of God.

The Old Testament writers were inspired to prophesy the coming of Jesus to the earth, while the New Testament writers became the biographers and eyewitnesses of His earthly visit. Both revealed the same Divine Person who has fulfilled every prophecy spoken of Him hundreds of years before He was born. More about this later.

The debate about Jesus' life centers around three basic concerns...(1) the historical reality of Jesus, (2) the virgin birth of Jesus, (3) the resurrection of Jesus. Let's begin our discussion with a look at the historical reality.

THE HISTORICAL REALITY OF JESUS

The question on some people's minds is... "Did Jesus really exist or was he just a myth concocted up by the Biblical writers?" In other words, is there any other proof beyond the Bible to confirm the existence of Jesus?

The first thing that you and I need to be aware is this... there is no debate among historians regarding Jesus' life. They accept Jesus as a true-life historical person. No serious scholar would risk any suggestion declaring the non-historicity of Jesus. Yes...there was a man named Jesus, who was born in Nazareth and who died by Roman crucifixion just as the Bible states.

With that all said, let's briefly review some of the reasons for scholars' rigid and uncompromising position.

For this study we will look beyond the early Christian sources confirming Jesus' historicity, i.e., beyond early church fathers (Justin, Irenaeus, Origin, Polycarp, etc)...to concentrate on non-biblical sources. In doing so, let's first look at a Roman historian (Tacitus) who referred to the death of Christ and to the Christians at Rome in his article dating around 80 AD.

In his article, Tacitus states..."Christus (Christ), the founder of the name, was put to death by Pontius Pilate, procurator of Judea in the reign of Tiberius; but the pernicious superstition, repressed for a time broke out again, not only through Judea, where the mischief originated, but through the city of Rome also." (Annals XV. 44.

Apparently, Tacitus wasn't too impressed with the great zeal of the early Christians, referring to their belief in Christ as a "pernicious superstition". And he certainly didn't appreciate the fact that this "superstition" had now spread to Rome itself.

Another later Roman historian (Seutonius) also didn't appreciate the Christian evangelistic zeal, as seen by his remarks to the Roman Imperial House... "As the Jews were making constant disturbances at the instigation of Chrestus (Christ), he (Claudius) expelled them from Rome." (Life of Claudius 25:4)

Again he said, "Punishment by Nero was inflicted on the Christians, a class of men given to a new and mischievous superstition." (Lives of Caesars 26:2).

63

Keep in mind that these "Roman" historians were "Romans" ...and it was "Romans" who crucified the Christ they were discussing. Rather than confessing to the Divinity of Christ, they were sheltering Rome's murder by suggesting the followers of Jesus to be of a "mischievous superstition".

But, what about Jewish historians? After all, didn't the Jews also take part in the arrest and crucifixion of Jesus? Here's what the Jewish historian (Flavius Josephus) had to say around the early second century..."Now there was about this time Jesus, a wise man, if it be lawful to call him a man, for he was a doer of wonderful works, a teacher of such men as receive the truth with pleasure. He drew over to him both many of the Jews, and many of the Gentiles. He was the Christ, and when Pilate, at the suggestion of the principal men among us, had condemned him to the cross, those that loved him at the first did not forsake him; for he appeared to them alive again the third day; as the divine prophets had foretold these and ten thousand other wonderful things concerning him. And the tribe of Christians so named from him are not extinct at this day." (Antiquities xviii.33)

Other historians and philosophers of the time following the death of Jesus also referred to Jesus in their writings (Lucian, Pliny, etc.) as do other manuscripts that have been discovered, i.e. Tertullian, Thallus, Justin Martyr, the letter of Mara Bar-Serapon, etc. Even the Jewish Talmud has its references to Jesus.

64

So, then, with all the external references from those not associated with, or followers of Jesus, the fact of his historicity is unchallenged. The person of Jesus did exist and was crucified on a Roman cross just as the Bible records it...and just as historians from that period of time concur.

THE VIRGIN BIRTH
OF JESUS

Even though the reality of Jesus' earthly existence is a proven fact...that does not, by itself, confirm the miraculous part of his existence. The Bible's revelation of a miraculous virgin birth is the beginning to Jesus' miraculous life. The question is, "Did it really happen the way the Bible says it did?"

I must tell you that in all my research on this matter, I have found no apologetical writer with a scientifically acceptable answer, nor have I found any viable argument against the virgin birth. The truth of the matter is...no one really knows whether or not Jesus was born of a virgin beyond what the Bible tells us.

Objections to the virgin birth attempt to discredit the Divine nature of Christ. Some argue that the story was tailored from Greek, Babylonian or Egyptian mythology, but that doesn't tie in with pagan myth, as no pagan hero is credited as coming from a virgin birth. While some pagan deities are described with unusual births, the myths talk of adulterous sexual relations between a god and goddess, or with an earthly woman.

I wholly accept the virgin birth of Jesus as an established reality. My acceptance is based on what I know to be true about everything else the Bible teaches, so it is not a difficult matter for me to accept the teaching regarding Jesus' virgin birth. If everything else in the Bible has been proven to be true, then why would I question this one event? I don't.

This leaves us with the most fundamental and crucial event in all the Bible...or, for that matter...in all the world...

THE RESURRECTION
OF JESUS

Nothing...absolutely nothing...is more important to our entire human existence than the resurrection of Jesus Christ from the dead. This one event, alone, is the evidence, the proof, the absolute assurance of Jesus' divinity and authority. It is the basis for trusting him as Savior and Lord. Without the resurrection we are left with just another human religious teacher and a Bible full of unsubstantiated miracles and myths.

The resurrection of Jesus from the dead is the one event that separates him from all other professed religious redeemers. It is the one event that elevates Jesus above and beyond every human being who has ever existed on the face of the earth.

The resurrection of Jesus helps us to accept the reality of a virgin birth. It helps us to accept the healing of a blind man, the walking on the water...the calming of a violent storm.

There is nothing more important to a person's eternal welfare than to resolve the truth of who Jesus is...which means, there is nothing more important than resolving the truth of his resurrection, the one event that validates His Divinity. At the heart of Biblical credibility is the person of Jesus...who claimed Divinity...and proved it by having authority over death.

Over the centuries there have been frantic attempts by non-believers to try and discredit the Bible's report regarding the resurrection. Those attempts center around a logic that such an event could not have occurred, since Jesus was just a man and no other man has ever done such a thing. But no one has yet to provide any evidence...only theories. The theories are (1) Jesus didn't really die on the cross, he just fainted, or (2) the body of Jesus was stolen by his followers from the grave to concoct the story of a resurrection. Neither theory makes any sense.

Did Jesus just faint on the cross and later resuscitate, to go hide in the desert? Get real! Anyone who knows anything about Roman judicial ritual knows that the Romans would not have allowed a criminal to come down off the cross without making certain he was dead. The sword in the criminal's side was the final required verification of death. So, what about the disciples stealing Jesus' body, burying it somewhere...and then going all over the Roman Empire preaching he was alive? If that happened, then they all died a martyr's death for a hoax.

Here's the facts! Jesus did resurrect from the dead, just the way the Bible reports it. This created a major problem for the political and religious authorities who then had to deal with the masses of people, who were now convinced that Jesus was telling the truth and their Messiah had been wrongly judged and crucified. To cover up their crime, the politicians and priests conspired to make up a false story...that Jesus actually was dead and his disciples had stolen his body from the grave. To make their story halfway believable, the officials suggested that the Roman guards had fallen asleep at their post. Their story had many loopholes and was never accepted by the people.

Consider this...it was an irreversible law of the Roman army that no one slept at their post. The punishment for doing so was death...no questions asked. It would have been foolish for any Roman guard (assigned to guard the tomb of Jesus) to go along with such a story, knowing that their superiors would have put them to death as punishment. N o guard was ever punished.

But, just suppose the guards actually fell asleep at the tomb of Jesus...how then could a few men have rolled away the huge stone that covered the grave entrance, so quietly, that they did not disturb one single guard lying asleep next to the grave?

But, just suppose the disciples were successful in doing that...what happened to the body of Jesus? Where did they hide Jesus' body so that no one in the Roman Empire could find it?

68

Would it not have been the top priority of the Roman government and the Jewish religious leadership to hunt down and find the body of Jesus? Imagine what would have happened if his body went undiscovered. People might actually believe he was God in human flesh! The Roman and Jewish leaders could not take a chance on that happening...if indeed the body had been stolen as they tried to report. But there was never an all out search by the Roman and Jewish officials to recover the body of Jesus. There never was one single disciple brought before the court to confess what they did with the body. Why?

Instead of being questioned by the Roman and Jewish leaders (once the body was discovered as missing) the disciples were left alone as they preached in public places to the masses of people...telling them that Jesus had resurrected...while the religious and political leaders looked helplessly on in amazement and fear. Why didn't the leaders arrest them for preaching a lie and stirring up the people? Because they knew a miracle had happened and that Jesus was the resurrected Savior and Lord.

If all of this had been a hoax...that the disciples did steal and hide the body of Jesus...why did no one in their group ever betray the hoax by revealing it to the authorities? Surely, at least one of those early disciples would not have given their life for a fantasy they knew to be false. After all, these were just ordinary men (fishermen and tax collectors) with an amazing message.

Where is the body of Jesus? Had the disciples stolen it from the tomb, where in the world would they have hidden it so that it would never be recovered? Would it not still be the top priority of every religion on earth to uncover the body of Jesus to prove that He was a hoax...if they really believed He was? The reality is, no one has ever looked...even from the moment of the disciples' cries ... "He has risen from the dead".

Had the disciples stolen and hidden the body of Jesus... to cover up a hoax that was started by a now dead man...why would they eventually suffer imprisonment, beatings and death for a lie? No one would willingly give up their life if they really had known that Jesus was a deceiver and hoax. Every disciple of Jesus could have been spared their sufferings and death by simply ceasing to preach that Jesus had resurrected from the dead. They could have lived to ripe old ages by simply turning over the body of Jesus to the officials...but no one did.

The disciples died for their teaching because they knew the truth ...Jesus was alive. They had seen him, conversed with him, and were being empowered by his Spirit to preach those things they knew were true. The evidence is overwhelming... Jesus did resurrect from the dead three days after his crucifixion just as the prophets, and Jesus himself, proclaimed he would do. This fact alone is proof of his Divinity...that Jesus was exactly who he claimed to be...God in human flesh.

Many outside sources have confirmed the credibility of the Bible's record, including its report of the resurrection of Jesus. No evidence has been presented in the last 2000 years to prove otherwise. The Book is real...straight from God's heart.

Two thousand years ago a man named Jesus walked on the earth...healing all manner of disease and teaching powerful truths of hope for our human family. The religious and political leaders killed him...not because of His rebellion against the state...but because of His message of love. Three days after His crucifixion, Jesus resurrected from the dead. Where is He now? According to the Bible, Jesus returned to heaven where he now sits at the right hand of the Father God, making intercession for all mankind. Jesus is the Lord of the universe and Head of his Church that he created, and which is under his watchful care.

The man, Jesus, was more than just a man. He was God, who came to earth to reveal our Creator's love and compassion. He is the central message of the Bible...to confirm the Bible's credibility, not only from the accuracy of the New Testament story, but also by the prophetical precision of the Old Testament regarding his life centuries before he was born.

The Old Testament prophets revealed Jesus' virgin birth, where he would be born, the date he would be born, and about many other events of his life, in precise detail...even though human beings do not possess the ability to look into the future.

71

The remarkable prophetical ability of the Bible continues to amaze scientists and historians. Every single prophecy has been 100% fulfilled as predicted, which demands an answer to the question...How could mere mortal men prophecy events that would occur centuries later?

How could mere men describe a method of punishment not yet been invented in their day (crucifixion on a cross)? How could they have even thought that someone would resurrect from the dead three days after they had died...when no such thing had ever happened before or thought possible? There can be only one conclusion...they wrote the words that God told them to write.

The Biblical prophecies do not end with the life of Jesus. The Bible record (completed around 95 AD) contains precise prophesies of political and religious events that have taken place throughout history since that time...from the date of Jesus' death and resurrection in the year 33 AD, up to and including things that have happened in our current generation. The ability of the Bible to see into the future with such remarkable and accurate detail is a powerful support that it is more than just a collection of human writings.

As a conclusion to this part of our study, let's look at some of the prophecies regarding the life of Jesus and some of those dealing with world events in the years and centuries following his life.

OLD TESTAMENT
MESSIANIC PROPHESIES

There are 69 major prophecies and 270 additional minor predictions in the Old Testament that reveal a coming Messiah to earth. Every major and minor prophecy was fulfilled in the life of Jesus Christ.

Throughout his ministry, Jesus identified himself as the true Messiah who was revealed by the Old Testament prophets. The implications of his testimony cannot be taken lightly.

"And beginning at Moses and all the prophets, he (Jesus) expounded unto them in all the scriptures of the things concerning himself."   Luke 24:27

"And he (Jesus) said unto them, "These are the words which I spake unto you, while I was yet with you, that all things must be fulfilled, which were written in the law of Moses, and in the prophets, and in the psalms, concerning me."   Luke 24:44

(Jesus said) "For had ye believed Moses, ye would have believed me: for he wrote of me. But if ye believe not his writings, how shall ye believe my words?"   John 5:46-47

The disciples of Jesus also referred to the Old Testament prophecies as confirmation that Jesus of Nazareth was the true promised Messiah. Throughout their writings they refer to him as God's Son, the Savior, and promised Messiah (Christ).

73

"And Paul, as his manner was, went in unto them, and three sabbath days reasoned with them out of the scriptures (Old Testament), opening and alleging, that Christ must needs have suffered, and risen again from the dead; and that this Jesus, whom I preach unto you, is Christ."   Acts 17:2-3

All of the prophesies of the Old Testament were written over a period of 1000 years, the last being recorded at least 400 years prior to the birth of Jesus. Skeptics attempt to discredit these facts by suggesting that the prophecies were written after the life of Jesus and fabricated to agree with the events of his life. The problem with that idea, however, is that the Septuagint (Greek translation of the Hebrew Old Testament) was translated between the years of 200-150 BC. In other words, there is a minimal gap of 200 years between the recorded Old Testament prophecies and the birth of Jesus.

The fact that there is such a large number of prophecies regarding the Messiah (that are so precisely specific)...there can be no error in recognizing the person who has fulfilled them... that person being Jesus. It has been calculated that the chance of one person fulfilling <u>only eight</u> of the prophecies spoken of him would be a 1 in 10^{17} (1 in 100,000,000,000,000,000) chance. Just imagine what the chance of fulfilling <u>all 69 major</u> prophecies would be...yet the historical Jesus of Nazareth has done just that. Modern-day researchers have now accepted that truth.

Here's a brief review of those Old Testament prophecies that identify the coming Messiah (which the life of Jesus has totally satisfied). To begin with, the prophecies identify the <u>exact lineage</u> through which the Messiah would be born...

A. Shem (one of Noah's 3 sons)

B. Abraham (from the Ur of the Chaldees)

C. Isaac (one of Abraham's 2 sons)

D. Jacob (one of Isaac's 2 sons)

E. Judah (one of Jacob's 12 sons)

F. Line of Jesse (from many family lines of Judah)

G. David (one of Jesse's 8 children)

The specifics of this lineage are remarkably precise, so as to define the exact person from the exact birth line whereby no mistaken identity could occur. Consider this...

Noah had three sons (Shem, Ham, Japheth) from which every race on earth is traced...but God eliminated 2/3rds of the possibilities for Messiah's lineage by selecting Shem. God later chose one man (Abraham) from the whole human race through which the Messiah would be born. How many other possibilities did this eliminate? From Abraham's two sons, God chose Isaac over Ishmael (eliminating ½ of that possibility) for continuing Messiah's bloodline. From Isaac's two sons (Esau and Jacob) God chose the younger Jacob (another 50% elimination) to further identify Messiah. And then Jacob fathered twelve sons.

God eliminated 11/12ths of Jacob's twelve sons in His choice of Judah for the continuation of Messiah's lineage…from which, out of all the many family lines of Judah's tribe, God chose the line of Jesse.

Jesse had eight sons from which God chose one (David) as the line of continuation for Messiah's birth, removing another 7/8ths of the possibilities…taking us up the line to a day when Mary, the mother of Jesus, gave birth to Messiah.

Get the point in all this? Of all the possibilities for a direct bloodline to Messiah's birth, only one could work out perfectly…and the Bible told which line it would be centuries before it ever happened. Could I use the word "amazing" here?

Did all this happen by coincidence? The mathematical probabilities are off the charts. There's no way to figure it. But this is just the beginning of prophecies regarding the Messiah.

Another remarkable prophecy (recorded in 1012 BC) is in regards to the Messiah's death by crucifixion. Not only did the prophecy reveal the unlikely way Messiah would die…it also described the Messiah's crucifixion 800 years <u>before</u> <u>the</u> <u>Romans</u> <u>invented</u> <u>crucifixion</u> as a technique of capital punishment.

A listing of the other Old Testament "Messianic" prophecies will help to put this all in perspective. As you look over them, keep in mind that Jesus has fulfilled every one in perfect detail.

OLD TESTAMENT MESSIANIC PROPHECIES

1.   Messiah would be born of a woman's seed
2.   Messiah would be born of a virgin
3.   Messiah would be born in Bethlehem
4.   A killing of infants after Messiah's birth
5.   Messiah's ministry would be proceeded by a messenger (John the Baptist)
6.   Messiah would be a prophet
7.   Messiah would have special baptism of the Holy Spirit
8.   Messiah would teach in parables
9.   Messiah would perform a ministry of miracles
10. Messiah would be a stumbling block to the Jews and a light to the Gentiles
11. Messiah would be betrayed by a friend and sold for 30 pieces of silver, which would be used to purchase a potter's field
12. Messiah's disciples would forsake him
13. Messiah would be accused by false witnesses, but would remain silent before his accusers
14. Messiah would be smitten, mocked and spit upon
15. Messiah would be crucified with thieves
16. Messiah would be rejected by his own people
17. Messiah would be hated without a cause
18. They would cast lots for Messiah's garments
19. Messiah would be given gall and vinegar to drink while on the cross of crucifixion
20. Messiah would be mocked while crucified
21. Messiah's side would be pierced
22. A darkness would cover the land at Messiah's death
23. Messiah would be buried in a rich man's tomb
24. Messiah would resurrect from the dead three days after his crucifixion
25. Messiah would ascend back to heaven after his resurrection, to be seated at right hand of God

When all these Old Testament prophesies are openly and objectively considered, there can be no question that they satisfy the criteria for the scientific conclusion…that the Bible is indeed a book of prophetical ability. And there is even more evidence.

NEW TESTAMENT PROPHESIES

There are two sources of New Testament prophecy, (1) the prophecies spoken by Jesus and (2) the prophecies given to John as recorded in the book of Revelation. The Revelation prophesies reveal the historical events that would affect the "true church that Jesus built", i.e. the true followers of Jesus. The time frame covered in this prophecy spans the "Christian era" from the time of Christ until the end of the world (the second coming of Christ). Revelation identifies the enemies to God's true church that would come in two forms. The first enemies were the pagan political adversaries (starting with the pagan Roman Empire) …who physically assaulted the followers of Christ. The second enemy would be false (humanly organized) "Christian" religious systems (Roman Catholicism, Protestantism) that would try to substitute for God's true church. The Revelation message, then, is…God's true church, its adversaries, and the church's victory.

Historical events of the last 2000 years have confirmed the remarkable accuracy of the Revelation's prophecy. It is an awesome book from the mind of God…to say the least. In another study, we help to unlock its symbolic mysteries.

PROPHECIES OF JESUS

During his ministry, Jesus made several predictions of future events...all of which have been fulfilled precisely as he spoke them. The only exception is the prophecy of his eventual return to earth that is yet to occur.

Two of his prophecies deal with signs regarding the time of his return...signs that involve the Jewish people and the city of Jerusalem. Both of these prophecies have been remarkably fulfilled (the latest in 1967 AD). Let's look at the first of these prophecies revealing the destruction of Jerusalem.

> "And Jesus went out, and departed from the temple: and his disciples came to him for to show him the buildings of the temple. And Jesus said unto them, See ye not all these things? verily I say unto you, There shall not be left here one stone upon another, that shall not be thrown down. And as he sat upon the mount of Olives, the disciples came unto him privately, saying, Tell us, when shall these things be? and what shall be the sign of thy coming, and of the end of the world?"   Matthew 24:1-3

Notice what was happening when Jesus made this prophecy. Jesus and His disciples were standing in front of the Jewish Temple in Jerusalem. As they stood there, Jesus made a profound declaration. He told his disciples that the temple would be totally destroyed (not one stone left on another).

79

Naturally, this came as a shock to the disciples. They asked Jesus when the destruction of the temple would happen. Then, they asked him two other questions. "When will you return to earth and when will the world come to an end?"

It is important to note that the disciples asked three questions. One, when will the temple in Jerusalem be destroyed; two, when will Jesus return to earth again; three, when will the world end? The disciples asked three questions and Jesus answered them in order. The confusion of some Bible students is to apply Jesus' answer only to His second coming, rather than considering that part of his answer dealt with events prior to the destruction of Jerusalem and the Jewish temple. Putting this in perspective will help to clear up the confusion.

Jesus declared, "All these buildings will be knocked down, with not one stone left on top of another!" This prediction was fulfilled in the year 70 AD (just 37 years after Jesus' death). At the time of this prophecy there were no wars, or rumors of wars. The world was at a temporary peace, including the Jews with the Romans. But that would soon change, just as predicted.

Josephus, a non-Christian Jew, was a leading historian of Jewish history immediately following the life of Jesus. In his historical account (War, book vii c1), Josephus tells the events of Jerusalem's destruction. His accounts correspond perfectly with the prophecy of Jesus.

According to Josephus, the temple was built of white and green spotted marble stones...some measuring as much as 50 feet long by 24 feet broad by 16 feet thick (Antiquities b.15.c.xi). Jesus' suggestion that not one stone would be left upon another was highly improbable...but it happened just as He said it would. The Roman army totally demolished the temple with the city.

Josephus, who was a Jewish priest, was taken captive and observed the entire siege and destruction first hand. In his account of the war, Josephus writes, "Caesar gave orders that they should now demolish the whole city and the temple, except three towers (Phaselus, Hippicus, Mariamne) and a part of the western wall and these were spared." (War, book vii.c.1) He also stated that, after the city was taken, "Titus gave orders to demolish the whole city and temple as Caesar commanded. Three towers were left standing, but for the rest of the wall, it was laid so completely even with the ground by those who dug it up from the foundation, that there was nothing left, to make those believe who came hither that it had ever been inhabited."

It is truly amazing that all this happened just 37 years after Jesus' prophecy...but he saw it coming and gave signs and warnings to his followers. Jesus predicted specific events that would occur prior to the fall of Jerusalem...covering the time span between the years of 33 AD (when Jesus was crucified) and 70 AD (when the temple was destroyed).

81

The destruction of Jerusalem in 70 AD began a series of events that would continue throughout history (up to 1967 AD) just as Jesus predicted...to give us a timetable of His second return to earth (that would occur sometime after 1967 AD).

The disciples had asked Jesus when the Temple and the city of Jerusalem would be destroyed. Jesus answered by giving them various signs they were to look for...all of which were historically fulfilled precisely as Jesus said they would. In another writing titled, "The Final Days Of Mankind", we look deeply into those signs preceding the fall of Jerusalem (70 AD).

Nowhere in history is there recorded a more violent assault on a people than that of Titus' army on the people of Jerusalem in 70 AD. Those in Jerusalem suffered horrible calamities and misery. Within the city walls were murder, famine, devastation and pestilence...while outside there was fire, sword and other horrors of war. The days of vengeance, recorded centuries before by the prophets, were now being fulfilled...just as Jesus also prophesied. Amazingly, the Romans burned the temple in the same month and on the same day of the month, as did the Babylonians centuries before. (Josephus, War, b.vi.c.4)

Just 37 years prior to this terrible devastation, the Jews at Jerusalem cried out at the trial of Jesus, "Crucify him, crucify him...let his blood be on us and our children". How horribly their chant was honored!

The final prophecy of Jesus was fulfilled in 1967 AD. It is referred to as the "pre-sign date" for his return to earth.

Although former teachers, living prior to the mid 20th century, were correct in declaring the imminent return of Christ, they didn't have a dated confirmation to declare Christ's return as soon at hand. But that all changed in 1967 AD...when the Lord's dated pre-sign of his return was finally fulfilled.

Two thousand years ago, Jesus revealed a <u>specific date</u> on which we could attach the final signs just before his return. That date, which we now know to be 1967 AD, is the basis on which we can now understand the final signs of his coming... realizing that we are now very close to our Lord's return.

The dated pre-sign deals with the recapture of Jerusalem by the Jewish people after 2500 years of Gentile (non-Jewish) control. This is a remarkable prophecy of Jesus. At the time he made this prophecy, Jerusalem had been under Gentile control for 500 years, with no reason to suggest that the Jews could ever again regain power. Even so, Jesus had the ability to see into the future (to the year 1967) to predict that the Jews would regain control of Jerusalem after 2500 years of Gentile domination.

Beginning with his prophecy regarding the destruction of Jerusalem in 70 AD, Jesus then continued to share events that would follow that destruction...events that spanned history all the way up to 1967 AD as a final timetable to our Lord's return.

In perfect detail, Jesus described the events that would take place after his death (33 AD) and before the destruction of Jerusalem (70 AD). Then he said... *"And then shall the end come"* ...referring to the fall of Jerusalem. That event (the destruction of Jerusalem 70 AD) was the first phase of our Lord's prophecy regarding his return to earth at a later time. Jesus, then, made a profound prophecy that escapes the casual reader...

"And Jerusalem will be trampled by Gentiles until the times of the Gentiles are fulfilled."   Luke 21:24

Jesus told his disciples that... *"When you see the 'abomination of desolation', spoken of by Daniel the prophet, standing in the holy place, then let those who are in Judea flee to the mountains."* That abomination was the non-Jewish Gentiles (Roman army) who entered the Temple in their siege of the city.

The Jewish temple was a sacred place for the worship of Jews alone. No Gentile (non-Jew) was permitted entrance into the temple's sanctuary. But that changed when Titus and his army overwhelmed Jerusalem in 70 AD.

The Romans are further identified as an "abomination" because of their pagan ensigns and images, which they brought into the Temple of God and placed at the city's eastern gate, where they made sacrifices to their pagan gods. This was an abomination to the Jews who worshipped the one true God in their Temple. But the Gentiles' abomination was not to last.

84

Jesus revealed the Gentiles' control of Jerusalem would not last forever, that the Jews would eventually regain power of Jerusalem...just before his return to earth. That prophecy came true in 1967 AD. The "Six Day War in 1967 AD confirmed the accuracy of Jesus' prophecy. The "time of the Gentiles" is now over. Jerusalem is now under the control of the Jewish people for the first time in 2500 years...just as Jesus prophesied.

This single event in 1967 AD is the dated pre-sign for the return of Christ. Those who anxiously anticipate His return now look for the physical signs, religious signs, and moral signs that Jesus revealed would follow the 1967 AD date, just before his return to earth. All of those signs have now been fulfilled, suggesting that our Lord's return is imminently soon.

IS THE BIBLE A CREDIBLE SOURCE FOR OUR ETERNAL QUEST?

You're the one to decide that for yourself but, as for me, I have enough empirical evidence from years of research to fully satisfy my belief...that the book we call the Bible is the only book with credibility...as God's divine revelation of Himself and His will to our human family.

Everywhere we look, reality just keeps getting better and better.

The Bible's Message...
A Miracle Of Timeless Wisdom
Even For Our Modern Day

This is one of those topics where the answer depends on who you talk to. What may be relevant to one person may not be all that relevant to another. That's why this chapter is rather short and dumb sounding. But you can't say I didn't warn you ahead of time.

Let's start this off by defining what we mean by the word "relevant". A check of the thesaurus whips up some words like "pertinent, applicable, important, appropriate, significant", but that doesn't say much...for, what is significant or important to one person isn't all that significant or important to another, so we're right back where we started. Asking the question, "Is the Bible relevant?" is better asked this way... "Does the Bible teach anything that is important or significant...to YOU?"

Some ministers might proclaim that the Bible is relevant for everybody...because they assume everybody wants to know who God is and everybody wants to go to heaven when they die. But that may not really be true. For some people, life is an involvment with other priorities and it's just not that important to know who God is right now. Also, heaven isn't that much of a real deal either, so it can wait until just before the last gasp of air.

So then, we get right down to the meat of it all. The Bible just "ain't" worth a whole lot unless you're interested in the stuff that it's teaching. But, isn't that true of every other book in the world? After all, who wants to read the instructional manual on "How To Milk A Cow" unless you've got one mooing in the back yard with a pouch full of milk?

Sound dumb? Think about it. No subject is important to a person unless it is important to that one person. And when it comes to things like God, religion, heaven and eternity...no person on earth is going to make these topics important to you. That's something you have to decide for yourself...and no, I'm not preaching...I'm just being up front and honest.

But it is strange that some people would suggest that the Bible isn't relevant...that the Bible has no significance in these modern times. That's like saying that there are no humans on earth with any interest in their eternal destiny.

Let's back up a second and review a couple things we've already learned. First of all, this book we call the Bible is totally credible in what it says...without error or contradiction. And even though it was written thousands of years ago, the Bible sheds such timely insights on human nature, world problems and human suffering that it could have just as easily been written this morning. There's something about this book that elevates it far above all other works of human literature. It just makes sense.

The Bible retains a perennial wisdom that is applicable to all generations, including this very moment in which we live ...if that is the kind of wisdom you and I want to understand for ourselves. There is no question that the true God of the universe is the author of the Bible, as well as its guardian and its endorser.

The Bible contains knowledge and wisdom that never grows old. It speaks to the heart and mind of every human need in every generation. There simply is no other wisdom anywhere in the world that can compare to the ageless wisdom of God's word. It is the only book ever written that has survived many generations...to remain a permanent fixture in human education.

By comparison, the average life of a best seller is 5 years while 75% of all books that are printed are thrown on the scrap heap in 90 days. Yet, the Bible continues to intrigue the minds of those who seek for truth...with readers increasing every year.

The Bible's strong appeal is due to its wisdom in relating to the basics of human experience, as no mere human acumen is capable of doing. It is the only credible source available to our human family that tells us who we are, where we came from, why we exist and what the ultimate outcome of our life shall be.

The continuing demand for the Bible is explained by the fact that it meets the deepest needs of all people, regardless of age, race or circumstance. It is the only universal book, capable of speaking to the needs of all peoples in every culture.

88

The Bible satisfies the basic needs and desires of our human family, and answers all the deep questions that would otherwise be hidden. It reveals how every individual can regain fellowship with our Creator...and it provides a hope that there is an eternal life beyond this present world.

Only in the Bible can we find the fulfillment for all our needs and solutions to all our problems...something that no mere human writing is capable of doing.

Is it relevant for today's world? I would have to say that in the world we are now living...the Bible is the only relevant piece of literature that makes sense.

Somebody once commented... "What this world needs is someone who knows what this world needs". That's exactly where the Bible steps in.

Everywhere we look, reality just keeps getting better and better.

The Bible's Message
Seven Stories
That Tell It All

There are seven events in the Bible that summarize the central message of what the Bible teaches. A review of these seven events is an ideal beginning toward a systematic journey in learning the fullness of the Bible's message.

There are many issues dealt with in the Bible, such as marriage and family, nutrition, psychology, etc. The central priority, however, involves our human existence...to answer questions of who we are, why we exist, our life's problems and their solutions...and ultimately, our eternal future. The seven Bible stories (events) that summarize our human situation are... (1) the creation (2) the fall of mankind (3) the great flood (4) the coming of the Messiah (5) the resurrection of Lazarus (6) the crucifixion of Christ...and (7) the resurrection of Christ.

The Creation...

The Bible reference for this event is found in the book of Genesis, chapters 1 and 2. There are two lessons taught in the creation story...(1) the natural universe and all things therein are a creation of the one Divine Being known to us as God and (2) human beings are a unique creation of God...for a very special and elevated purpose in God's plan.

Genesis is the book of beginnings. It tells the beginning of the physical universe, as we know it, including our earth and all things thereon. It appropriately begins with the declaration, *"In the beginning God..."*

The message of the Bible, beginning in this first verse and continuing throughout the book, is that God is the beginning, the end, and the fulfillment of all things. It is in God that we live, breathe, and have our being. The Bible makes no attempt to prove the existence of God, it only reveals Him. God's existence is not a Biblical argument...it is an accepted fact. This is also true of the creation story. It simply states that God is the Creator of all things. Mankind has no existence beyond God.

There are many evidences beyond the Bible that prove God's existence and His active involvement in human life. Science further confirms the universe to be an instantaneous creation rather than an evolved event. While the Biblical creation account was not intended to be a treatise on science, its harmony with biological and zoological knowledge is well accepted. Scientific discovery does not contradict the creation account. In fact, the more we learn through science, the more the creation story is confirmed. This is also true of all other Biblical truth.

The final creation of God was His most impressive. God created a living human being "in His image". No other creature of God was so created...or so privileged.

91

The Bible uses the term "man" on several occasions to identify the whole of "mankind", including male and female. The term "man" is translated from the Hebrew "adam" (pronounced aw-dawm), meaning…"a human being, the species of mankind, an individual, a person" (sex excluded).

> "And God said, Let us make man in our image, after our likeness: and let them have dominion over the fish of the sea, and over the fowl of the air, and over the cattle, and over all the earth, and over every creeping thing that creepeth upon the earth. So God created man in his own image, in the image of God created he him; male and female created he them."   Genesis 26,27

Man (woman) is a special creation of God with particular qualities above those of other creatures…

1. Human beings are the only creation of God that was made "in God's image".

2. Human beings are the only creation of God to possess a living "soul".

Humans possess special gifts that the animal world does not possess. As creatures made in God's image we have the ability to think, to reason things out, to plan and make decisions. We are capable of loving, of feeling emotion, and of acting upon thoughtful logic based on collected input, while the animal world functions on instinct at a given stimulus without logical thought.

Humans were also given a "living soul" that will live forever, unlike the animal world that ceases to exist when they die. This further set humans apart as unique and superior creations of God...identifying every person on earth as having infinite worth and equal value to his or her Creator. We are each a special creation of God, made in His image with gifts, abilities and the special privilege of being allowed fellowship with our Creator. This is the Bible story of the creation.

The Fall Of Mankind...

The Bible reference for this second event is found in the book of Genesis, chapters 3 and 4. It reveals the failure of our human family and the cause of all human problems here on earth. It is the story of "sin"...i.e. human rebellion against the supremacy and authority of our Creator.

There are several lessons taught in the Bible on the topic of sin. It is obvious from the great amount of discussion on this topic that God wants us to fully understand what many people prefer to avoid, or try to ridicule as being insignificant.

The Bible teaches us (1) the definition of sin, (2) the origin of sin, (3) the two-fold nature of sin, (4) the consequences of sin, (5) the punishment for sin, and (6) the solution to the sin problem. In another book titled, "The Problem With God And Evil", we deal with the sin topic at length, while in this study we will only take a quick preview.

Adam and Eve were the first to rebel (sin) against God and to experience the terrible consequences for their rebellion. Since then, all human beings have followed in their footsteps, as the Bible reveals... *"We have all sinned and come short of the glory of God."* Every human has failed his or her Creator...but none of us really want to hear that, do we?

The reality of sin answers many questions about life, even though many people try to avoid or deny its existence. The Bible makes a very pointed and powerful declaration in defining sin (rebellion against God) as mankind's only problem. The simple truth of our human existence is that...if sin were totally abolished on earth, there would never again be another problem of any kind. The world would be a perfect place to live.

The word "sin" is mentioned 447 times in the Scriptures. The Hebrew and Greek words (chatta'th and hamartia), translated in the English as "sin", both mean "an offense or trespass"...i.e. to disobey or rebel against the commandments of God.

The consequence of man's rebellion is seen in every area of human existence. Credible scholars acknowledge sin to be the root cause for mental and physical illness, social breakdowns in marriages and families, civil unrest, crime, hunger, homelessness and all other human maladies. From a Biblical perspective, sin is the primary problem that mankind must deal with...to suggest that, if sin were abolished, all human problems would disappear.

94

For some modern thinkers, this fundamental Bible truth is an oversimplification to the complex issues that we face in our world...yet, mankind has no alternative solution for resolving the tragedy of human life to which we are exposed. While some have tried to substitute other human theories for human behavior, the Bible is more straightforward in identifying man's rebellion against the authority of our Creator as the sole culprit.

> "... by one man (Adam) sin entered into the world, and death (consequences) by sin; and so death (consequences) passed upon all men, for that all have sinned..."   Romans 5:12

It took only two chapters of human history for sin to be revealed, but the disturbing question is...why? Why did Adam and Eve rebel against God? They had everything they needed. They lacked nothing. Adam and Eve were given control over their environment and all earthly creatures, yet they gave in to the temptation to do the one simple thing God had commanded them not to do. Why? And why have you and I rebelled against our Creator...the One who is most concerned about our welfare?

The Bible's answer to the "why" question is defined as "human pride". Adam and Eve wanted to be "gods". They did not want to be under the authority of a higher power other than themselves. This was their error and the error of humanity ever since. Mankind wants to control his or her own destiny without the intrusion of a higher power. But that cannot happen.

95

The Bible teaches that we are either under the control of a righteous God or an evil devil. No human being is independent from the spiritual forces around us, although much of our human family is not willing to accept that reality. We have all inherited a false pride that eventually causes us to rebel against the laws of our Creator...the consequences of which include bondage to the world of evil spirits.

Adam and Eve's character became corrupted as a result of relinquishing control of their life to Satan (the evil spirit). While some people wish to dismiss this suggestion, the Bible is emphatic in declaring that there are only two choices we have in life...(1) to serve God or (2) become a servant to Satan.

The punishment for our "sinful rebellion" is two kinds of "death" ...spiritual death and physical death. Before their sin, Adam and Eve were eternal beings who could have lived in the Garden of Eden forever, without ever experiencing physical death. But, because of sin, mankind now suffers mortality...and since the time of Adam and Eve, no person has survived physical life for very many years. Because of our rebellion (sin), there is an eventual and absolute end to physical life, as we know it.

A second kind of death is identified in the Bible as "spiritual death"...meaning that we no longer have a relationship with our Creator. Because of our rebellious sin, God has turned away from us, to no longer be in fellowship with us as a friend.

Physical death occurs when we are separated from life while spiritual death is a separation from God...which means, a person can be physically alive and spiritually dead at the same time. We may be enjoying life but, if we are still sinners, we are not enjoying God's fellowship.

The punishment for Adam and Eve's sin was expulsion from the Garden of Eden and from God's presence. Adam and Eve could no longer fellowship with God. Life on earth and life in eternity, without God, is sin's ultimate punishment. The Bible does, however, offer hope for human beings, which we will look at later, but first...

The Great Flood...

The Bible reference for this event is found in the book of Genesis, chapters 4 through 9. There are several lessons taught in this story...(1) the depth of human depravity as a result of sin, (2) the consequence and certain judgment for sin, (3) God's mercy and willingness to deliver mankind from sin's consequences, (4) a confirmation of the Bible's authenticity and accuracy.

It didn't take long for sin and human depravity to reveal itself after the fall of Adam and Eve. Life on earth quickly turned cruel as Adam and Eve's son, Cain, murdered his own brother.

This murder was just the beginning signal of a corrupt human race that continued to worsen in succeeding generations, to the point that God finally said...enough is enough.

97

The moral condition described in Genesis (chapter 6) is a tragic picture of how sin had corrupted our early human family. Human morality had become so debased that it grieved the Lord He had ever created humans. In fact, God was so grieved that He determined to destroy mankind from the face of the earth by a great worldwide flood.

Fortunately, there was one person (Noah) who was seen as righteous (non-rebellious) in the eyes of God, and because of Noah's righteousness, God not only spared Noah and his wife, but also Noah's three sons and their wives as well. These eight people would begin a replenishment of the human population on earth after God's judgment had destroyed the wicked.

The flood of Noah's time reveals the propriety of God's justice. It reveals a God who not only punishes evil but who also rewards the good. One without the other could not be considered as equitable or unbiased justice.

God saw the human moral condition in Noah's time as so perverted that the thoughts and the intents of their hearts were continually wicked. Nothing good could be seen in the conduct or character of our human ancestors. Because of this moral disgrace, God determined to destroy the human race with all its wickedness and perversion. But even while God's justice was proper and definite...His mercy was also fair in rewarding the righteousness of Noah and his family, by sparing their lives.

Noah's family was spared from the flood by an ark built from God's blueprint. The ark was about the size of a present day ocean liner (450' long, 75' high, 45' wide). It had three decks and one door in the side, with a row of windows around the top. Noah's ark was built of gopher wood, a species of wood no longer in existence. Once the floodwaters receded, the ark of Noah came to rest on the top of Mt. Ararat. This mountain range of Armenia is 17,000 feet high and mostly inaccessible due to its glacier vastness...but something very interesting has been going on for the last several years.

Just prior to the Bolshevik revolution, Russian airplane pilots began to report seeing the hulk of a gigantic ship covered in ice high in the regions of Mt. Ararat. But about the time of these sightings, the atheistic Bolsheviks overthrew the Czarist government, so that these reports were never made public until recently...after new sightings promoted more investigation.

Explorers have now made the incredible journey to reach the site of this huge, ice-encased, ship. Analysis of the wood samples reveals the species to be that from which the ark was made. In addition to the onsite investigation, there are also high altitude photographs with computer analysis, confirming the ship still buried deep in the ice of Mt Ararat, as being the remains of the original ark of Noah. This amazing discovery is just another, of many confirmations, to the validity and truth of the Bible.

After the Ark was built, God commanded Noah and his wife, along with their three sons and their wives, to load up the ark with seven pairs of clean animals and one pair each of unclean animals. It has been calculated that there was room in the ark for 7000 animal species, as well as the eight remaining human beings...from which all future generations of animal and human life would continue. After closing the door, God allowed no other earth dweller to enter the ark. He then sent a worldwide flood to destroy all remaining living creatures.

Noah and his family lived in the ark for one year and seventeen days. The first five months they were floating while the last seven months they waited in the ark on Mt. Ararat for the floodwaters to recede. At the end of the year, God ordered them to disembark to start a new world, giving His promise that the earth would never again be destroyed by a flood. As a sign of that promise, God placed a rainbow in the sky...to remind us every time it appears that God's promise is still intact.

Noah's sons (Shem, Ham and Japheth) migrated from the mountain of Ararat to repopulate the earth. Ham, whose name in the Hebrew means "burnt", was apparently so named because his complexion was more darkly tinted than his brothers. Migration to the south, where Ham's descendents adapted to the hot and sunny climate, made Ham the father of the black race...whose future enslavement to the other races was prophesied by Noah.

100

Shem's descendants migrated to the east, where they gave birth to various eastern cultures including the Hebrew (Israelite, Jewish) people, in fulfillment of Noah's prophecy that they would be "the preservers of the knowledge of the true God". It was these Hebrew descendants who preserved the knowledge of God throughout Old Testament Biblical history.

The prophecy of Noah regarding Japheth's descendants (the Caucasian race) was that they would inhabit a larger portion of the earth and would replace the Semitic race as teachers of God. This prophecy was fulfilled when Jesus was rejected as the Messiah by the Jewish people and accepted by the Caucasian Gentiles who, as Christian believers, became teachers of God's truths, replacing the Semitic religious teachers.

The story of the great flood is a tragic example of our human history that began as special creations in God's image, only to deteriorate into rebellious and humiliated reprobates. It is a history of rejection toward God's authority...and even after the flood, mankind has not learned our lesson...to persist in the tragic path of rebellious disobedience toward our Creator.

But, as the Bible story continues, it is the goodness and mercy of God that has stepped forward to intervene in behalf of human failure and weakness. No event in all of human history remotely compares with what our Creator has done in our behalf. No greater love has ever been expressed to our human family.

101

The Coming Of The Messiah...

The fourth event described in the Bible is the one where God's mercy takes control to resolve the problem of human sin. It is the birth and life of Jesus, the Christ (Messiah), who came to earth as the doorway through which you and I may enter into a personal relationship with God. Jesus said it this way...

> "I am the door: by me if any man enter in, he shall be saved, and shall go in and out, and find pasture. The thief cometh not, but for to steal, and to kill, and to destroy: I am come that they might have life, and that they might have *it* more abundantly."
>
> John 10:9-10

The significance of Christ's birth and his life is beyond the capacity of humans to convey to one another. It is an event of profound blessings that can only be experienced (individually) in response to God's gift of love...which He sent to us from heaven in the person of His only begotten Son.

The perplexing problem we are faced with as individuals is how to overcome the power of evil that has control of our life, and how to avoid the consequences and ultimate punishment for our sinful rebellion against our Creator.

How can you and I avoid being destroyed by sin...now that the power of Satan is the dictator of human life? This is the most urgent and perplexing question in all of human history.

102

There is no scientific, social or political answer for the problems of mankind...as continually evidenced in almost every news report. Our human family has tried to find substitutes for God...searching for answers to our problems through our limited human resources...but no answers are to be found. We humans are totally helpless and perplexed in our search for a solution to the problem of sinful rebellion...and to the pain and suffering which that rebellion has created for our human family.

Fortunately, God has not left us alone to fight the battle. He has provided a solution for anyone who will respond. This brings us to the heart of the Bible story, where God's method for solving our sin problem is revealed through Jesus, the Messiah. It is in the fullness of Jesus where God's mercy and love are fully expressed...even while we were yet sinners.

The Bible reveals Jesus Christ to be much more than just a historical celebrity who lived some 2000 years ago. It reveals him to be the Son of God, who existed in heaven before he came to earth. Jesus is part of the Divine Godhead, whose earthly visit in human form was for the purpose of helping us resolve our sin problem. When he finished his work on earth, Jesus returned to heaven where he now lives as our intercessor.

The questions of Jesus' historicity and Divinity have been settled long ago for anyone who desires to search for truth. The reality of Jesus is no longer an issue for debate.

The birth of Jesus, the Christ, is recorded in the first several chapters of the New Testament books (Matthew, Luke). The events surrounding his birth and his life are miraculous and indisputable…since every part of his life was prophesied in exact detail hundreds of years before He was born.

God had long been telling the world through different Old Testament prophets that the Messiah would be coming. One revealed the Christ would be born of a virgin…a miraculous conception that no other woman on earth will ever experience. Another prophet identified Messiah's exact genealogical lineage; another announced Bethlehem to be Messiah's birthplace, while another revealed the exact date when Messiah would be born. There were also prophecies regarding the massacre of infants and the flight into Egypt, all of which were fulfilled in the life of Jesus…to reveal a specific baby's birth that was far beyond coincidence. God wanted to make certain that the world knew exactly who His son was, so that we would have complete faith in the One chosen of God to solve our sin problem.

There have been many false, self-proclaimed saviors throughout history who promised great things for those who followed them. None of the fake saviors delivered on their promises. The only exception is the real Messiah sent from the real Father God. Jesus said it this way…

> "I am the way, the truth, and the life: no man cometh unto the
> Father, but by me."   John 14:6

The Resurrection Of Lazarus...

This brings us to a fifth event described in the Bible... the resurrection of Lazarus, which is recorded in the eleventh chapter of John's gospel.

The earthly life of Jesus lasted about thirty-three years, beginning as a child in the home of Mary and Joseph, until he began his public teaching and healing ministry at age thirty. Keep in mind that Jesus had no "formal" religious education to prepare him as a Jewish religious teacher...but even as early as age twelve, he astounded his listeners with the wisdom and deep spiritual insights that his possessed. People could not understand where this young boy could have gained such wisdom for, as yet, they were not aware that God in the flesh was speaking to them.

During the three years (age 30-33) of his public ministry, Jesus healed various kinds of illnesses and performed many miracles. The Gospel writers list some of his miracles while acknowledging that Jesus performed many more that they have not recorded. One of the miracles, however, that they made certain to give an account, was the reviving of Lazarus back to life...after he had been dead and buried four days.

There were two other occasions where Jesus raised a dead person back to life (rich man's daughter and the son of the widow at Nain), but the resurrection of Lazarus was unique in that he had been dead so long and already buried in his tomb.

Jesus had made acquaintance with Lazarus and his two sisters, and regarded by them to be a close friend. No one knows, but it could be possible that Lazarus and his sisters were friends of Jesus as far back as childhood...but that is just thinking out loud with no Biblical support. Whatever the case, Jesus was a close family friend as revealed by the sister's attempts to let Jesus know that Lazarus was ill.

While he was ministering in another city, Jesus heard the news of Lazarus' death and decided to return to where he was buried. When Jesus arrived (four days after Lazarus had died) he met with the grieving family and friends at the tomb...where he gave instruction for the tomb to be opened. Some questioned his request, but Jesus knew that He had the power to bring Lazarus back to life. Once the grave was opened, Jesus called to the dead Lazarus to come forth...and the dead man walked out of the tomb to the amazement of all who witnessed it.

This was not the only dead person Jesus brought back to life during His earthly ministry, but in this particular story Jesus made a profound and important declaration to our human family. It is the most encouraging statement of hope that you and I will ever hear...ringing loudly even today for everyone who will believe. Jesus declared...

> "I am the resurrection and the life. He that believes in me, though he were dead, yet shall he live. And whosoever lives and believes in me shall never die."   John 11:25-26

106

This declaration of Jesus summarizes the whole message of the Bible and is the purpose for why the Bible was written. It reveals God's desire for all human beings (including you and me) that we enjoy an eternal life (to live forever) even when our physical life on this earth has ended.

This declaration and miracle of Jesus reveals the power of God and His willingness to deliver us from the consequence and punishment of our sin. It is telling us, that even though you and I have sinned, we have a hope of being restored to God's fellowship and of enjoying eternal life with God after this life is over. Can there be any greater message than that?

The first chapters in man's history are about human failure and the problems we have created for ourselves because of our rebellious sin against our Creator. But the final chapters of man's history are about God's love and mercy, and about His willingness to help us conquer our sin through His gift of salvation…a gift offered through His only Son, Jesus.

The Crucifixion of Christ…

This brings us to the sixth Bible event…the crucifixion of Jesus. Each of the four gospels in the New Testament has something to share about the trial and crucifixion of Jesus. Matthew (beginning chapter 21), Mark (beginning chapter 11), Luke (beginning chapter 19), and John (beginning chapter 12) all share various events surrounding Jesus' death and resurrection.

107

The accounts of Jesus' cruel trial and crucifixion provoke the question, why? Why did Jesus have to suffer the indignity and pain? Why did he allow human beings, who he had created, to arrest, mock and crucify Him as they did?

At any moment throughout his ordeal, Jesus could have called on the heavenly angels to come and deliver him from the hands of his captors, yet Jesus did not do so. His suffering was for a higher purpose than the pain he suffered. Jesus suffered and died a cruel death so that you and I could live. He came to this earth to die for our sins so that you and I would not have to be punished. The physical pain and death that Jesus suffered, however, were not his greatest torture.

Jesus experienced a suffering that you and I will never fully understand It was revealed by what he said in the last moments while he was hanging on the cross... *"My God, my God, why have you forsaken me?"*

The supreme sacrifice that Jesus paid, by taking our sins upon himself, was to be punished...not only by physical death, but by <u>spiritual death</u> as well. For the first time in all of eternity <u>Jesus was spiritually separated</u> from his heavenly Father. With our sins upon his shoulders, Jesus was now the sinner who God could no longer fellowship with. As he hang upon the cross of Calvary, Jesus experienced for the first time in his existence, that God had turned His back upon him as a sinner.

We cannot comprehend the difficult and tragic decision that God had to make as He looked upon Jesus as a sinner with all the sins of the world upon him. Your sins and mine were on the shoulders of Jesus as he hung there on the cross. It was your sins and mine that made God turn His face away from His only Son. The sins of all mankind caused God to forsake His only Son for the first time in all of eternity. Tragic!

Jesus died a spiritual death that day on Calvary's cross, so that you and I could have spiritual life. He was rejected so that you and I could be accepted. There is no greater sacrifice that God could have given for our human family...no greater love than what Jesus expressed in doing what he did for you and me.

The religious community refers to the day Jesus died as good Friday, but there was nothing good about it. It was a black and tragic Friday when God sacrificed His only son because of our failures. It should never have had to happen. Jesus should not have needed to be punished. Jesus didn't commit sin, we did.

Why did God send His innocent, righteous Son to a world full of sin and evil, to experience the pain and humiliation that Jesus suffered? The answer is...God's holy character and perfect sovereignty demanded justice be served on the rebellious defiance of a subordinate creation. Someone must be punished for the arrogant contempt toward God's authority. The creation cannot be allowed to challenge the Creator.

Our rebellious crime against the authority and integrity of our Creator is so severe and offensive to His moral reasoning that there is nothing man or woman can offer in restitution. We are totally guilty and helpless in the court of God's justice.

But, in His mercy, God offered His Son as the sacrificial restitution for our sinful rebellion...the only sacrifice that will bring honor to His name. Nothing in the universe has more value to God than His only begotten Son. Nothing in the universe can satisfy the integrity and righteousness of God as punishment for the sins against His authority.

Jesus suffered and died the way he did as the punishment for your sins and mine...because there is nothing we could offer that would satisfy the Creator of the universe. Jesus came to earth to resolve our sin problem once and for all...thanks to his obedient love, and the love of the Father. The only explanation for the death of Jesus is that it happened because of love. God loved us so much that he allowed His son to die for us...

> "For God so loved the world, that he gave his only begotten Son, that whosoever believeth in him should not perish, but have everlasting life. For God sent not his Son into the world to condemn the world; but that the world through him might be saved. He that believeth on him is not condemned: but he that believeth not is condemned already, because he hath not believed in the name of the only begotten Son of God."
>
> John 3:16-18

110

The Resurrection of Christ...

The event of Christ's crucifixion is not the end of the story. Three days after Jesus was put to death on Calvary's cross, he came back to life...to live forevermore. Jesus is alive, and because he forever lives, you and I have the hope that we will live forever as well.

Physical death is not the final chapter in the lives of our human family. There is a world beyond this life where Jesus has gone to prepare a place for those who love Him...

"Let not your heart be troubled: ye believe in God, believe also in me. In my Father's house are many mansions: if it were not so, I would have told you. I go to prepare a place for you. And if I go and prepare a place for you, I will come again, and receive you unto myself; that where I am, there ye may be also."   John 14:1-3

The resurrection of Jesus is the finale of God's work in our eternal salvation. The failure of mankind that began way back in the Garden of Eden is now overshadowed by the victory of Jesus.

Sin is no longer life's master for those who have placed their trust in God's eternal salvation through Jesus, the Christ. The power and consequence of sin has been defeated, as we are more than conquerors through Him who loved us. What greater message is there in life than that? We win because of Jesus!

111

The only tragedy that remains in our world is that there are yet too many people who have not accepted God's wonderful love and salvation. As a consequence, many of our human family are still enslaved to their sin...without hope in this life, or for the next life that is just around the corner.

The tragedy remains, that even after all God has done to assure our eternal destiny, many are still blinded by the devil's temptations just as Adam and Eve were many centuries ago.

We can only pray and hope that the rebellious members of our human family will come to the full understanding of what life is really all about. This is the message of the Bible and why the Bible was written.

Everywhere we look, reality just keeps getting better and better. Thanks to God!

A Summary Of
The Old Testament Teaching

In this chapter we will take a quick tour through the Old Testament, to lay a foundation for more in-depth studies. In my opinion, this is the place to begin a systematic study of the Bible.

The first five books of the Old Testament (Genesis, Exodus, Leviticus, Numbers, Deuteronomy) are known as the Pentateuch (meaning five), so designated as the books written by Moses. They are also referred to as the "Law Books", as they contain God's Old Testament law with the Ten Commandments.

The next twelve Old Testament books (Joshua through Esther) are known as the "Historical Books", as they provide a historical record of the early Israelite (Hebrew, Jewish) people. The "Poetry Books" (Psalms, Proverbs, Ecclesiastes and Song of Solomon) contain private meditations of their writers and are read for personal inspiration and worship.

The last seventeen books (Isaiah to Malachi) are named for God's prophet who wrote them. These books deal primarily with the political situation of the nation of Israel, to prophesy events that occurred long before the birth of Christ. Intermingled in these Old Testament political prophecies are other prophecies that promise a coming Messiah (Christ) who would establish his spiritual kingdom.

The Israelites misinterpreted the Messianic prophecies, believing the prophecies promise a <u>political</u> savior rather than a <u>spiritual</u> savior. They expected their Messiah to deliver Israel from their political enemies, and to set up an earthly political kingdom...but Jesus (God's true Messiah) didn't fulfill their expectations (to become their political liberator from Roman oppression). Consequently, Jesus was rejected as the Messiah and punished as a troublemaker, while the Jewish people still look for their political Savior who they believe is yet to come.

The Book Of Genesis...

The word "Genesis" means "origin" or "beginning". The first part of Genesis (first 11 chapters) tells of four major events...the creation, the fall of man, the flood, and the Babel crisis. The second part (chapters 12 thru 50) covers the life of four people beginning with Abraham, Abraham's son (Isaac), Isaac's son (Jacob), and one of Jacob's twelve sons (Joseph).

The first two chapters of Genesis describe the creation of the natural universe, as we know it, beginning with the phrase, *"In the beginning God"*. Although the Bible was not intended to be a book of science, it does reveal many things of scientific interest that have come under a great deal of scientific scrutiny. But the more that science explores the Biblical account of the creation, the more it has found the Bible account to be a reasonable explanation for the beginning of life.

114

As to the existence of God, the Bible declares there to be one eternal God who has manifested Himself to the human race in the form of three Divinities…God, the Father; God, the Son; and God, the Holy Spirit.

Chapters three and four deal with the topic of sin. In these chapters we learn what sin is, why humans commit sin, and the consequences for sin. These are disturbing chapters, for they reveal the failure of our human family and the underlying reason for all human problems.

Chapters five through nine reveal the extent of God's patience with sinful rebellion, as well as God's grace that is willing to forgive. The worldwide flood was the result of man's ongoing rebellion and deteriorated character. The question for some is, did the flood actually happen, or is it just a Biblical myth? The answer is, the flood did happen, and is confirmed by modern scientific studies.

After the flood, Noah's sons drifted to different regions where they began new families to replenish the earth, but man has a short memory. In chapters 10 and 11, the rebellious nature of mankind once again rears its ugly head as man attempts to reach heaven to become his own god. God foiled the attempt by confusing their language. The "Tower of Babel" was a memorial to their failure. Later in history, where the tower of Babel stood, the Babylonian empire was created and named (today's Iraq).

115

Chapter 12 begins the history of the Hebrew (Jewish) people, who play a monumental role in the remainder of Biblical history. The Jewish nation began with Abraham, a man selected of God to father a chosen nation, from where the Messiah would eventually be born...who would bless all nations on earth.

Abraham, at a very old age, fathered two sons (Ishmael and Isaac). Isaac was born of Abraham's wife (Sarah) while Ishmael was born of Sarah's handmaid (Hagar). Ishmael became father of the Arab (Palestinian) nations, while Isaac continued the lineage of Abraham as the father of the Jewish (Hebrew, Israelite) nation.

Both these nations (as descendants of Abraham) claim to be God's chosen people...but God's chosen people, to who Gods promises were given, were those through Sarah's son, Isaac (the Jewish nation). Isaac also fathered two sons (Esau and Jacob) but only Jacob was selected to carry the lineage through which the Messiah would eventually be born. Later, Jacob's name was changed to Israel, from where the nation of Israel received their identity. The Israelites are also referred to as Jewish or Hebrews.

Jacob (Israel) fathered twelve sons who later became known as the twelve tribes of Israel. Jacob's special love for one of his sons (Joseph) created jealousy among the brothers, who sold Joseph as a slave to the Egyptians. This act initiated the eventual enslavement of all of Israel's children to the Egyptians.

The Book Of Exodus...

The history of God's chosen people (Israelite nation), took a tragic turn in Egypt for 400 years before God delivered them from slavery, to reestablish their nation. The book of Exodus picks up the history of the Israelites in Egypt and their deliverance from slavery...to their promised land of Canaan.

God had previously revealed to Abraham that his seed would spend 400 years in Egypt, also promising that He would deliver them from their captivity. The person who God called for the task was Moses (chapters 1-3). Through God's miraculous power in bringing a series of plagues upon the Egyptians, Moses was able to convince the hard-hearted Pharaoh to release God's people to return to their own country.

The trip from Egypt to the "promised land" was not an easy one for the children of Israel. Their first challenge was in crossing the desert that separated Egypt from their homeland, a journey that should have taken only a few days, but ended up lasting forty years. During their forty-year desert wandering, the Israelites received God's Old Testament laws on tablets of stone (summarized in the Ten Commandments). Later, God gave the Israelites a blueprint for a worship tabernacle along with specific instructions of religious ordinances...that included the Jewish priesthood and a redemption process through the blood sacrifices of sheep and goats...as a prototype of Christ's blood redemption.

117

The tabernacle was a large tent that could be moved and reassembled during the Israelites' desert journey. It became the pattern for a permanent worship temple once they had settled in their homeland and capital city, Jerusalem.

The Book Of Leviticus...

The law given to Moses on Mt. Sinai and later detailed in the book of Leviticus was a forerunner to the New Testament law of Christ. Jesus declared his law was not a replacement for Old Testament law, but rather an expanded, in-depth spiritual expression. We'll look more into the relationship between the Old and New Testaments in the next chapter.

Leviticus gets its name from one of the twelve tribes of Israel (Levite) who were chosen of God as the priests (ministers) to the rest of the nation of Israel. No priest could be ordained from any Israeli tribe other than the tribe of Levites. In all future generations, the priesthood of the Jewish people have been from the Levite tribe. The only exception, which was ordained of God, was that the one Great High Priest (Messiah) would not be born through the lineage of the Levites, but rather would come through the tribe of Judah (Genesis 49:8-10).

In so doing, God has set the true Messiah apart from all other prophets and priests...so that no prophet, priest or person can be confused with the true Messiah. The genealogy of Jesus has fulfilled this requirement as God's true Messiah.

118

The book of Leviticus gives a detailed explanation of Gods laws, showing Israel how to live in fellowship with God. It details the sacrificial system, the precepts of the law and the penalties for violation. Leviticus can be divided into two broad sections…(1) the way to God through animal sacrifices (chapter 1-17) and (2) how to walk with God (chapter 18-27).

Leviticus details the Burnt offering; Meal offering; Peace offerings; Sin offering, and the Trespass offering…all of which have been replaced in the New Testament by the one offering of Jesus (the Christ) on Calvary. Chapters 8-10 define the consecration of the priests and high priests. Aaron (Moses' brother) became the first high priest to the nation of Israel while Aaron's sons became the first priests.

The 11th chapter has special significance even for today, as it describes clean and unclean foods that are good and bad for human consumption. This list of foods provides an outline for healthy eating that has been proven to be beneficial if obeyed.

One important lesson to learn from the teachings of the Bible is the emphasis it has on prevention rather than therapy. God's advice is offered as preventative medicine…to help us maintain mental, physical and spiritual health. He prefers for us to remain healthy rather than to frantically search for healing. This preventative approach is no more graphically illustrated than in the nutritional chapter of Leviticus (chapter 11).

Chapter 23 defines various feasts of significance, to be observed by the Israelites at different seasons...i.e. the Feast of Passover, Feast of Unleavened Bread, Feast of First Fruits, Feast Of Pentecost, Feast of Trumpets, Day of Atonement and Feast of Tabernacles. These feasts were designed to help the children of Israel in their walk with God. But, like the animal sacrifices and ordinances of the Old Testament, these feasts are not required for mankind's salvation or with our walk with God. They have been replaced by God's salvation plan as revealed and provided through Jesus, the Christ.

The Book Of Numbers...

This book gets its name from the Greek word, Arithmai, so named because of the numbering of the children of Israel... which was done twice.

Numbers takes up where Exodus left off, with just one month between the two books. The Leviticus instructions were given in between. The forty-year journey of the Israelites in the wilderness desert continues in the book of Numbers, where a census is taken...as the old generation dies off and replaced by a new generation.

Many events described in the book of Numbers are often referred to in the New Testament, making this one of the more important Old Testament historical reference books in providing background material to New Testament teaching.

The Book Of Deuteronomy...

The book of Deuteronomy is the last of the five books (Pentateuch) recorded by Moses. Deuteronomy derives its name from the Greek "deuteros" (meaning "second") and "nomos" (meaning "law"). In this book we have a second giving of the Old Testament law that was first described in Leviticus.

Deuteronomy was intended as a new presentation of the law for the new generation of Israelites who had grown up in the wilderness. It is not a new giving of a new law, but rather a more explicit detail of that which had previously been given.

The Book Of Joshua...

The first five books of Moses lead the children of Israel up to their promised Canaan land. The book of Joshua leads them from their desert wanderings into the "Promised Land". The remainder of historical books (Joshua thru Esther) covers Israel's history inside their Promised Land.

The first five chapters of Joshua talk of Israel's entering into Canaan. Joshua, who has been commissioned of the Lord as Israel's leader, has replaced the now retired Moses. Chapter two describes an amazing miracle (the fall of Jericho's massive walls) to allow the Israelites success in conquering the city. The story tells of how that God caused the Jericho walls to fall down as the Israelites marched around it while blowing their trumpets. This attack plan was devised by God himself.

121

Recent archaeological discovery of the sight has brought about some amazing revelations. The walls of Jericho fell in an opposite direction to the normal landscape. In other words, had they fallen because of an earthquake, as some skeptics suggest, they would have fallen downhill with the landscape. Instead, the walls <u>fell uphill</u> against what would be normal. God performed this miracle to help the Israelites in the conquest of the promised land...that was, at that time, inhabited by idolatrous heathens.

God promised the Israelites that He would help them if they followed His instructions explicitly. Unfortunately, the Israelites disobeyed God's command and, as a consequence, they suffered a devastating defeat in another battle. But, once they repented of their disobedience, the Israelites again continued in their conquest to gain control of the land that God had promised to Abraham centuries before.

After gaining control of the country, the Israelites then divided the land among their twelve tribes. They were now in total control because of God's fulfilled promise to Abraham. As long as Israel trusted God to be their sovereign leader, they were assured of remaining in control of their land...but as Jewish history unfolded, we see how future Jewish generations became unaligned with God...turning away from God to worship idols. The tragic history of the Jewish people reveals the consequences of rejecting the God who had delivered them from slavery.

Joshua, the military leader who helped in delivering the children of Israel into their promised land, is considered a "type" or "shadow" of Christ, the spiritual leader who delivers all of mankind into a fellowship with God. The name "Joshua" is the Hebrew word for the Greek word "Jesus" (meaning "deliverer" or "savior").

The Book Of Judges...

Judges takes its name from the book's contents. After the death of Joshua, the people of Israel commissioned judges from among themselves to be their military and spiritual leaders. It was a sad period of Jewish history during which time the nation compromised with idolatry. The Bible speaks of this time as a people who *"did evil in the sight of the Lord"*.

Because of their spiritual compromise with idols, God removed His protection, allowing Israel to be delivered into the hands of their enemies...that began with the Mesopotamians, then the Moabites, Canaanites, Midianites, and Philistines. At each defeat the Israelites repented to seek God's help, which He responded to by sending liberators in the persons of Othniel, Ehud, Deborah, Barak, Gideon, Jephthah and Samson.

Repeatedly, the Israelites seemed to learn their lesson by repenting and returning to the Lord...but their rebellious pattern continued until, later in their history, the nation of Israel was totally destroyed and their land controlled by their enemies.

123

The Book Of Ruth...

The book of Ruth belongs also to the historical period covered by the book of Judges and is named for its heroine, Ruth. It is one of only two books in the Holy Scriptures that bear the name of a woman...the other being the book of Esther.

The Books Of Samuel, Kings And Chronicles...

These three double books are the record of the rise and fall of Israel's monarchy. After a period of Judges the Israelites wanted a King to rule over them (like other nations) and sought God to give them one. They were, in effect, saying to God that they preferred an earthly leader who they could see rather than the invisible God who had continually delivered them from their slavery and their enemies.

God obliged Israel's request by selecting Saul to be the first of Israel's Kings. But Saul, being only a man, soon revealed his human weaknesses. Saul was an impatient, rebellious, hostile and jealous man...ultimately plotting an unsuccessful murderous death of David. Saul's ultimate decadence was in turning to witchcraft and, finally, suicide.

The successor of Saul to Israel's throne was David, who reigned forty years in both triumph and trouble. David began as a righteous and successful king but, because of sin, his triumphs turned to tragedy. During David's reign the city of Jerusalem was selected to be the capital seat of Israel's government.

After David's death, Solomon (David's son) assumed power as Israel's King for the next forty years. At Solomon's death, the united Kingdom of Israel became divided into two kingdoms (Judah and Israel).

The united kingdom of Israel lasted for three kings (Saul, David, Solomon) under which all the twelve tribes of Israel were unified. The ultimate division of the twelve tribes took two tribes one way while ten tribes went the other. The ten tribes retained the identity of "Israel", settling in the northern region, with Samaria as their capital. The other two tribes, "Judah", claimed the southern region, with Jerusalem as their capital. During the history of the two nations (Israel and Judah) various kings over both nations came to power...some of which showed integrity and honor in following the one true God, while others were dishonorable to follow after idols.

The northern kingdom of Israel lasted for about 250 years, during which time a total of nineteen kings reigned over them. The southern kingdom of Judah lasted for about 390 years under the reign of twenty kings.

Opposing governments eventually overthrew both Israel and Judah, taking them into captivity. The northern Israelites were overthrown by the Assyrians while the southern nation of Judah lasted another 140 years before being captured by the Babylonians, thus ending the sovereignty of the Jewish nation.

The Books Of Ezra, Nehemiah, Esther...

This brings us to the books of Ezra and Nehemiah that describe the return of a small remnant of Jewish people back to Jerusalem from their captivity, to restore their city and temple that had been destroyed by the invaders. The book of Esther deals with those Jews who stayed in the land of their captivity, rather than to return to their homeland.

This is one of the most important topics in Jewish history...the return of the Jewish people to their homeland after the Babylonian captivity. Under Ezra and Nehemiah the walls of Jerusalem and the temple were rebuilt, with the deposed people of Israel once again resettling in their homeland. With these two books (Ezra and Nehemiah), the record of Israel's Old Testament history comes to a close. A general understanding of this history is important for Bible students in understanding the teachings of the New Testament.

The Prophecy Books...

The final Old Testament section contains the books of prophecy (the prophet's name identifying each book). The Bible uses the word "prophet", not only as one who reveals the future, but also as someone who speaks in behalf of God. Bible prophets spoke both to the current events of their day and, on occasion, were also given the ability to speak of future events. They acknowledged their message as coming directly from God.

126

There are two different types of prophecies revealed in the seventeen Old Testament prophetical books. The first were warnings to Israel and Judah, at different times in their history, to alert them of their rebellion against the one true God and the consequences they would suffer by ignoring God's prophets. The prophets' warnings were not heeded...the result being, that both Israel and Judah succumbed to foreign aggression, a history that continued up to the 20th century.

The second series of prophecies announced the Messiah (Savior) who would appear on earth at a future date. The precise accuracy with which the Messianic prophecies were recorded is truly remarkable. The history and writings of the Old Testament occurred hundreds and thousands of years before the birth of Christ, yet they reveal intimate details of Messiah's earthly life long before his appearance. And every prophecy was fulfilled precisely in the life of the historical Jesus of Nazareth.

There can be no question regarding the Bible's ability to see into the future, or that the Jesus of the New Testament is the true Messiah from God (identified by the Old Testament prophets centuries before he came to earth). Both the Old Testament and New Testament reveal events that would occur in the future...events that only an omniscient God could have known beforehand...and revealed to His prophets who recorded them precisely as they were received from God.

127

The Silent Years From Malachi
To The New Testament...

Malachi is the last book of the Old Testament, written some 400 years before the birth of Jesus, to leave a silent record of history not included in the Bible. A look at those 400 years of Jewish history from other sources can help to better understand some of the opposition to Jesus' earthly ministry.

The Assyrians destroyed the northern kingdom of Israel in 722 BC. Later, in 587 BC, the Babylonians took the southern kingdom (Judah) into captivity. When the Medo-Persian Empire overthrew Babylon, an order was issued for the Jews to return to Jerusalem and build their worship temple. This order was carried out under Zerubbabel in 515 BC. Ezra restored worship in the temple and later, under Nehemiah's leadership, the city walls of Jerusalem were rebuilt. But the Gentiles were in control.

This was the situation of the Jewish people at the beginning of the 400 silent years. A small remnant had returned to Jerusalem, restoring the Jewish temple and worship...but the masses of Jews still remained captive in foreign countries. It is this small remnant, returning to Judah, who preserves Jewish history between the Old and New Testaments. During those 400 years, there were six different periods of foreign rule, beginning with the Persian rule over Palestine, and lasting until Alexander the Great and his Greek Empire came to power in 333 BC.

During this period, the translation of the Old Testament from the Hebrew to the Greek language was achieved. This translation is known as the "Septuagint". The death of Alexander resulted in Judea falling into the hands of the Egyptians.

The most tragic period of the inter-testament era, for the Jews, came when Palestine fell into the hands of the Syrians. The reign of Antiochus Epiphanes (beginning in 175 BC) brought terror on all the Jews. Antiochus devastated Jerusalem...tearing down its walls and killing the people. He desecrated the Jewish worship temple in every possible way, to offend both the Jews and God...the most serious offenses being the offering of a pig on the altar of sacrifice and the erection of statues of false gods.

The atrocities of Antiochus Epiphanes motivated a group of Jewish dissenters, who were led by Mattathias (an aged priest) and carried on by his son (Judas Maccabeus). This was one of the most heroic periods in all Jewish history, during which time Judas Maccabeus led in the restoring of the temple and the return of worship. When Judas Maccabeus was killed in a battle with the Syrians, his brother Jonathan became the military leader and high priest, uniting the civil and priestly authority in one person.

This began the Hasmonean line of Jewish high priests that continued through successive leaders, until the Herod family appeared on the scene, bringing an end to the Maccabean period and a beginning of the Roman period.

129

Judea became a province of the Roman Empire in 47 BC by Julius Caesar's appointment of Antipater as controller of the region. Antipater then appointed his son, Herod, to be governor of Galilee...then later as king of the Jews. This was "Herod, the Great" who was king when Jesus was born.

This short summary of the political events during the 400 silent inter-testament years reveals some events that had a great impact on the Jews. Political changes, however, were not the only things that affected the Jewish community.

There were also changes in Jewish religious customs, as new religious groups (Scribes, Pharisees, Sadducees) and new religious institutions (the Synagogue and the Sanhedrin) were created.

The Pharisees believed that the "Oral Law" was given orally to Moses, then to Joshua, to the elders, to the prophets and then to the men of the Great Synagogue. The Pharisees were the interpreters of the Oral Law during the time of Jesus, and later devoted to the written Talmud (still used in Judaism today).

The Sadducees disputed the Oral Law, believing that the only religious law of the Jews was the Pentateuch. They rejected the spirit world of angels, immortality, and the resurrection of the dead...while the Pharisees accepted all these doctrines. Needless to say, these two religious groups were in constant opposition to one another.

Another religious group, known as the Scribes, was developed around the time of the Babylonian captivity. This new line of Scribes not only transcribed the scriptures, they also had become the expounders, guardians and teachers of them as well. The scribes were a highly distinguished order within the Jewish nation...but Jesus denounced them because of their corruption and outward piousness.

There is no mention of synagogues in the Old Testament although they are mentioned throughout the New Testament. The synagogue did not exist before the captivity, but seems to have originated during that period of time, as the Jews attempted to separate themselves from the idolatry of their guardians. It is believed that the synagogue came into being from the desire of the Jewish people to have the scriptures read to them, since their adversaries had formerly destroyed the temple. These readings in the synagogue were commonplace at the time of Jesus. It was from this background that the early Christian church took on its form of worship. Titles given to New Testament church leaders (elders, bishops, deacons) were carried over from the synagogue.

The Sanhedrin, another Jewish tribunal in the early New Testament era, was composed of a high priest, 24 chief priests, 24 elders, and 22 scribes. This group interpreted both religious and civil law as the governing panel for the Jewish nation. It was the Sanhedrin who ordered the crucifixion of Jesus.

This brief background identifies some of the institutions established during the 400 silent years, and which were still in existence during Jesus' life and ministry. Various references in the New Testament confirm these Jewish groups that came into existence after the writings of the Old Testament.

We now have a basic (although brief) foundation for deeper Bible studies. Once Biblical history is understood, then the Bible is open to explore other questions and direction, about life, that we may seek for answers. The Bible has something to say on every relevant topic involving our life's circumstance, and can be a most helpful reference for almost every situation. Much of its wisdom is hidden, however, without a basic knowledge of the historical events we have just briefly reviewed.

We have learned in this lesson that the Israelite nation (also known as Hebrew and Jewish) plays an important role in Biblical history. It also plays a role in understanding the spiritual lessons that God intended for our human family. This nation of people began with the lineage of Abraham, Isaac, Jacob and Judah...through which the Messiah would later be born who would bless all nations of the world. It was a nation of ups and downs, but still surviving from centuries of abuse and aggression by foreign nations. It all goes back to a faithful God who made a promise to Abraham. Everywhere we look, reality just keeps getting better and better.

A Summary Of
The New Testament Teaching

The New Testament centers around the life and teachings of Jesus Christ. The first four books (Matthew, Mark, Luke and John) are known as the gospels, meaning "good news". They are so called because they tell the good news that God's Messiah, who the Old Testament had been predicting for many centuries, had arrived at long last.

The gospel of Matthew is the logical place to begin our New Testament studies, since the purpose of Matthew was to link the Old and New Testaments together, by identifying Jesus as the fulfillment of Old Testament prophecies concerning the Messiah. Mark and Luke continue a historical view of Jesus. Mark portrays him as the "servant Christ" by recording twenty of Jesus' miracles in detail, while Luke portrays the human side of Jesus by linking his condescension from a heavenly throne to human flesh. The gospel of John is a study of Jesus that stands alone, to climax the full purpose of God in Christ.

The four gospels are the most significant part of the Bible...more significant than the rest of the books in the whole world put together. These four gospel books contain a revelation that is more important to our human existence than any other knowledge or wisdom available to the human race.

133

The book of Acts continues New Testament history by recording the activities of Jesus' early followers in the immediate period following his death and resurrection. Two of these early followers (Peter and Paul) became very powerful and influential spokesmen of Christ's message.

The four gospels and the book of Acts provide us with more than just a historical knowledge of Jesus and His early followers...they also share the teachings of Christ on many topics relevant to human existence.

The next fourteen books of the New Testament (Romans thru Hebrews) are known as "Pauline epistles". These are letters written by the apostle Paul to the Christian congregations and associates that he had ministered to in his travels. Other letters written to early Christians from other disciples of Christ (James, Peter, John, Jude) are also included in the New Testament. These different letters (epistles) were inspired of God, and teach many profound truths and practical guidance for our daily lives.

The last book of the New Testament is the Revelation. This book of prophecy reveals the political and religious events that would affect the followers of Christ throughout the history of the true Christian church. Most of the Revelation prophecies have already been fulfilled, from the time of Jesus up to this present time, with one final prophecy yet to be fulfilled...the second coming of Jesus to the earth to reclaim his followers.

The Revelation has been a source of speculative teaching throughout the ages, but it isn't as complicated as some suggest. Its message is clear and its prophecies precisely fulfilled, making it a remarkable confirmation of the Bible's divine validity. God alone could have looked into the future with such remarkable accuracy, to reveal the events recorded in the Revelation.

The one thing that becomes abundantly clear throughout New Testament teaching is that, the historical Jesus of Nazareth is the sole fulfillment of God's plan for the eternal salvation of all mankind. The Bible emphatically declares that forgiveness from sin, and a restored fellowship with God, are possible only through what Jesus, the Christ has done for mankind.

THE GOSPELS

The first three gospels (Matthew, Mark and Luke) are known as "synoptic" gospels, providing a shared view (synopsis) of Jesus' life and ministry. The fourth gospel (John) reveals the deeper, divine Jesus in communion with God.

The four gospels provide credibility for the accuracy of historical reporting. The four offices of Christ (King, Servant, Son of Man, Son of God) are well defined in the four accounts. But, while the gospels are accurate, there are deliberate gaps in their reporting of Jesus' life...specifically in the eighteen years between the age of twelve and thirty, which none of the gospel writers deals with in their records.

135

John further states that... *"And there are also many other things which Jesus did, the which, if they should be written every one, I suppose that even the world itself could not contain the books that should be written."* (21:25)

While all four gospels fully agree with one another in their historical content, each writer was inspired of God to reveal different aspects of Jesus. The emphasis in Matthew's gospel is on the "Kingship" of Jesus...focusing toward Jewish thinking. In doing so, Matthew identifies the royal genealogy of Jesus (through King David), and the Sermon on the Mount (Jesus' kingly manifesto with the Laws of his Kingdom).

The emphasis of Mark's gospel is on the "Servant" role of Jesus in meeting the needs of humanity, as Mark appeals more to the Romans' way of thinking. Since the Romans were more impressed with works rather than words, Mark reported more of Jesus' miracles than did the other gospel writers. Mark also evaded the genealogy of Jesus, since the Romans had no interest in the background of a "servant".

Luke's emphasis is on Jesus as the "Perfect Man". His gospel, with a focus toward the Greeks, takes Jesus' lineage back to Adam (first man) rather than to Abraham (Jew). Luke shows Jesus in prayer (ministered to by Angels) as the "perfect man".

John's gospel clearly emphasizes the divinity of Jesus (Son of God) beginning with... *"In the beginning was the Word (Jesus) and the Word was with God and the Word was God"*.

The Book Of Matthew...

Matthew (a Jew) worked as a tax collector for the hated Roman government, collecting taxes from his fellow Jews before deserting his vocation to follow Jesus. God used this converted Jew to record the first gospel with a central message that can be summarized in his recurrent phrase, _"that it might be fulfilled"_.

The Jewish people of that day were well trained in Old Testament scripture, and especially the prophecies that revealed their coming Messiah. If they were to be impressed by someone, it would have to be a fellow-Jew who was well acquainted with the Old Testament and with Jewish customs. For a Jew to accept Jesus as the Messiah, they would have to be convinced that he fulfilled the Old Testament prophecies regarding Messiah. This is where the gospel of Matthew steps in.

Matthew continually refers to the Old Testament to show how Jesus of Nazareth fulfilled the prophecies. He, along with Luke, record the birth and early childhood of Jesus, while Mark and John begin their gospels at Jesus' entrance into the ministry.

All four of the gospels narrate some similar and some different incidences throughout Jesus' life and ministry, with one exception. They all record the arrest, trial, crucifixion and resurrection of Jesus in precise detail...including Matthew.

These final events in the life of Jesus are the ultimate message of the gospels...revealing the whole purpose of Jesus.

137

The glaring questions, however, about the cruel trial and crucifixion of Jesus are…"Why was Jesus crucified at the hands of his human accusers? What had Jesus done that deserved the punishment he received?" Jesus didn't promote anti-government sentiment in his teachings, nor had he collected an army to threaten the Roman government.

Jesus was not an evil man who perpetrated crime. He was not a threat to society. Jesus did not endorse a pagan religion to be a threat to the Jehovah God who the Jewish people honored and worshipped. So, what was Jesus' crime that they killed him?

The only thing that Jesus did in His earthly ministry was to go about healing the sick and teaching things that would make people's lives better. So, why did public sentiment go against Jesus, to punish him as they did? The answer is found in the Jewish religious leadership of that day, who became jealous of Jesus' popularity and power.

Jewish theologians had misinterpreted Old Testament prophecy regarding the Messiah…looking for a political savior to deliver their nation from their political enemies. Jesus didn't fulfill those expectations, but was still admired by the common people. Jesus was a threat to the established religious leaders, who had become corrupted with power, wealth and prestige. It was the Jewish ministers who falsely accused and brought wrong punishment to Jesus at the hands of the Roman government.

But there was another reason for Jesus to die as he did... a reason of more significance than human jealousy. The death of Jesus had been predetermined and ordained of God Himself, even before the world began.

Jesus was sent to earth as the supreme sacrifice to satisfy God's requirements for the forgiveness and justification of our sinful rebellion against our Creator. This is the primary message throughout the New Testament, beginning with the gospel of Matthew...that Jesus died for the sins of mankind.

The Gospel Of Mark...

Mark (also a Jew) was a companion of the apostle Paul on some of his missionary journeys. He also was a close companion of Peter. His description of Jesus' earthly life is from a somewhat different viewpoint than that of Matthew. While Matthew identified Jesus as the Christ by showing how he fulfilled Old Testament prophecy, Mark identifies him as the Christ by the works that He performed. Matthew directed his focus toward the Jewish mind and Mark wrote primarily to the Roman mind.

The Romans knew nothing about the Old Testament, so they had no interest in prophecy. They were more interested in a God capable of meeting their needs, rather than in a God who has Sovereign authority over the affairs of mankind. After all, the Romans were the world leaders...they didn't want a boss.

The word about Jesus had gotten around the Roman Empire by word of mouth, so the Romans were deeply interested in knowing more about the person who had appeared in Palestine with a remarkable gift of healing. Their interest was in knowing what kind of person Jesus was, and about the things he had done, and about the things he had been teaching. The gospel of Mark addressed their curiosity.

Twenty of Jesus' miracles are detailed in Mark's gospel, showing Jesus as the "Servant" to all mankind. In doing so, Mark revealed Jesus as a person of "deed" and "good works" ...rather than as just another self-proclaimed "deity" with cute words, weak solutions and an empty medicine cabinet. Mark's central message is summarized in chapter 10:45...

"The Son of Man came not to be ministered unto, but to minister, and to give His life a ransom for many."

The Gospel Of Luke...

Luke was the only one of the gospel writers who was a Gentile (not a Jew). He was a well-educated Greek equipped to write to the Greeks. As a physician, Luke was also a man with an intense devotion to the facts. The historical preciseness of his Gospel and book of Acts (which he also wrote) is well respected by scholars. Luke portrays Jesus as the "perfect man", the ideal example of manliness. The theme of his gospel was that Jesus came to seek and to save the lost as the "Son of Man" (19:10).

140

Luke uses the phrase, "Son of man", in dealing with the humanity of Christ and his human kindness toward the weak, the suffering and the outcast. But, while acknowledging the human side of Jesus, Luke does not fail to identify Jesus as "God in the flesh". In doing so, we are given a picture of a divine Christ who has sympathy and feelings for struggling humanity.

The Gospel Of John...

There is no mistake in John's gospel that Jesus was a unique person, far beyond all other human beings. He begins his gospel with this explicit and powerful description of Jesus...

"In the beginning was the Word, and the Word was with God, and the Word was God. The same was in the beginning with God. All things were made by him; and without him was not any thing made that was made. In him was life; and the life was the light of men. And the light shineth in darkness; and the darkness comprehended it not. There was a man sent from God, whose name was John (the Baptist). The same came for a witness, to bear witness of the Light, that all men through him might believe. He (John, the Baptist) was not that Light, but was sent to bear witness of that Light. That was the true Light, which lighteth every man that cometh into the world. He was in the world, and the world was made by him, and the world knew him not. He came unto his own, and his own received him not. But as many as received him, to them gave he power to become the sons of God, even to them that believe on his name: Which were born, not of blood, nor of the will of the flesh, nor of the will of man, but of God. And the Word was made flesh, and dwelt among us, (and we beheld his glory, the glory as of the only begotten of the Father,) full of grace and truth. John (Baptist) bare witness of him, and cried, saying, This was he of whom I spake, He that cometh after me is preferred before me: for he was before me. And of his fulness have all we received, and grace for grace. For the law was given by Moses, but grace and truth came by Jesus Christ. No man hath seen God at any time; the only begotten Son, which is in the bosom of the Father, he hath declared him."   John 1:1-18

John's gospel makes it clearly obvious that Jesus was God in human form. The Deity of Jesus is the focal point of John's gospel...where more of Jesus' teachings are documented than are the things Jesus did. Some have called John's gospel the most important literary production ever composed. The power of its teaching transcends all knowledge.

John's emphasis was to convince the Jews that Jesus was the Christ and to convince the Gentiles that Jesus was the Son of God. He exalts Jesus' divinity and character to be far above all human flesh and weakness. In every chapter, the deity of Jesus is disclosed...from Nathaniel's confession (Chapter 1), to the commandment "follow me" (chapter 21). Divine titles given to Jesus in John's gospel include "Word, Creator, Only Begotten of the Father, Lamb of God, the Great I AM".

John says of his writing, that it was written so that we might believe Jesus Christ was God. In his gospel, John records some startling claims that Jesus made of himself, i.e. that he was equal with God (5:17) and eternally existent with God (8:58).

Jesus also said of himself, _"I am the bread of life; I am the good shepherd; I am the resurrection and the life; I am the light of the world; I am the way, the truth and the life; I am the true vine"_. In support of these claims, John records some of Jesus' miracles that God alone could do (turning water into wine; the feeding of 5000; walking on water; healing a blind man; raising Lazarus from the dead).

Witnesses to all of these events testified throughout the Roman Empire...turning the world upside down with the reality that God had visited the earth in the form of a human being.

The last sermon of Jesus (chapters 14-16) and his last prayer for his followers (chapter 17) are the most encouraging words a human being could ever read. I highly recommend these chapters as the focal point of your continuing study activities.

The three persons of God's Trinity (Father, Son, Holy Spirit) are revealed in Jesus' final sermon. It is God in the person of the Holy Spirit, who becomes the inner, abiding guide and strength to the followers of Jesus. And even today, in a confused and treacherous world, God's Spirit continues to be our strength and Counselor. God's people are not alone. We are the victors!

The four gospel writers were personally and intimately associated with Jesus, as well as being associates with the other disciples of Jesus' inner circle. For that reason, the historical accuracy of the gospels is assured...confirmed by other historical writers (Christian and non-Christian alike) who lived and wrote at the time of Christ.

The four gospels reveal Jesus in his complex form (both as God and as human). Although it is difficult for the human mind to fully comprehend how the God of the universe could come to the earth as a human being, the separate gospel accounts provide the assurance that He did. In looking at the life, ministry and teaching of Jesus, it is difficult to conclude anything other than the reality that Jesus was, and is, truly God.

The resurrection of Jesus from death is the culminating historical event described by all the gospels. This event alone demands our acceptance of Jesus as more than just another human being. The resurrection of Christ is the single most important event in all of human existence, confirming Jesus to be the true Savior for all mankind. The resurrection of Jesus sets him apart from all other religious leaders and self-proclaimed saviors who have come and gone over the centuries...but whose physical remains still rest in their graves as a reminder that they were merely human flesh. The grave of Jesus is different. An empty tomb is the solid proof of the one, true, risen Savior.

The Acts Of The Apostles...

Luke recorded the "Acts Of The Apostles" as a historical continuation of events that immediately followed the life, death and resurrection of Jesus. As the title suggests, this book records the activities of Christ's first disciples, as they went forward into the then-known world to share the message of a risen Savior.

The diligent efforts of these early disciples succeeded in taking the gospel of Christ from Palestine to Antioch...and then westward through Asia Minor and Greece...and, finally, to Rome...to fully cover the heart of the Roman Empire. The fact that these eyewitnesses of Jesus' life were so diligent to share his story at great personal sacrifice (including martyrdom), speaks a powerful message to the truth of Christ. No one would give so sacrificially to a cause they knew to be a hoax. The life and resurrection of Jesus is well defended by the relentless effort of his followers, who made certain to carry his story to the world.

Although labeled the Acts of the Apostles, the book focuses on the outreach of Peter, and on Paul's unique ministry to the Gentiles (nationalities other than Jewish). Throughout the Old Testament we are assured of God's mercy to all peoples of the world (Jew and Gentile alike). The special calling of the Jewish nation was that, through that lineage, the Savior would be born for the blessing of all nations. Jesus Christ fulfilled that promise...bringing salvation and hope for all mankind.

145

This good news that Messiah had come was now being shared with the Gentiles, beginning with the ministries of Peter and Paul. The book Of Acts closes with Paul's two-year imprisonment at Rome. Paul was eventually beheaded for his testimony of Christ sometime after Luke recorded the Acts.

The Book Of Romans...

The apostle, Paul, shares his most complete explanation of the Gospel in his letter to the Christian converts at Rome... where Paul had not yet visited at the time of this letter.

The early Roman "church" was composed of Christians who had migrated to Rome from various parts of the East, some of who were Paul's converts and intimate friends. For future studies, let's clarify the Bible term, "church". It is a term that is translated from the Greek word "ecclesia" meaning "a called out assembly". In other words, the "Church of God" is a "called out assembly (group)" of God's people who have been saved from their sins (called out, born again).

> "And the Lord added to the church daily such as should be saved (born-again)."   Acts 2:27

The "church" at Rome was a group of Christ's followers (born again) who were assembling together for instruction, prayer and encouragement. The Bible "church" (of God) was not a formal religious organization as some think of it today.

There was a mixture of both Jewish and Gentile converts in the church at Rome at the time of Paul's writing. That mixture of backgrounds meant that there was also a mixture of beliefs.

The Jewish Christian converts maintained a strong belief in the Old Testament Mosaic Law as their guideline for God's will. The act of circumcision and following the Law of Moses were assumed to be requirements of the Christian faith by most Jewish converts...who further insisted these requirements be observed by the Gentile Christian converts as well. The question of whether a Gentile could be a Christian without becoming a Jewish proselyte was one of the great problems of that time. Christianity had started out as a "Jewish religion" and some powerful Jewish leaders were determined to keep it that way.

In addressing these misconceptions, Paul boldly declares that human justification before God rests solely upon the mercy of Christ, rather than on the Law of Moses. He argues the point that humans, in our sinful nature, cannot fully live up to Mosaic law to earn our salvation, and that only through Christ and the goodness of a merciful God, can we be forgiven of our sins.

The summary of Paul's letter to the Romans is that a relationship with God does not stand on what mankind has done, or can do, but rather on what Christ has done for us. Therefore, Christ is entitled to the unconditional allegiance and devotion of every human being on earth...Jew and Gentile alike.

147

The Two Books Of Corinthians...

Paul's first letter to the church at Corinth deals with some existing church disorders among the believers there.

Corinth was a commercial metropolis of Greece as one of the largest, most important cities of the Roman Empire. The commerce of the world flowed trough its harbors...as did many of the vices of the East and West. Paul ministered for one and a half years at Corinth, establishing a strong Christian church right in the midst of paganism and idolatry. But, three years after Paul left Corinth, a delegation of church leaders went to Ephesus (where Paul was ministering) to consult Paul about some serious problems that had arisen within the Corinthian church. In response, Paul wrote his first letter to deal with church factions and confusion on issues of immorality, lawsuits, meat offered to idols, abuses of the Lord's supper, false apostles, problems within marriage, disorderly conduct in their assemblies, women's part in the church and heresies about the Resurrection.

The Corinthian church, like Rome, had converts from various religious backgrounds (primarily pagan) whose earlier beliefs were in total opposition to the teachings of Christ. Being difficult to abandon, the converts reconciled old beliefs to their new Christian religion. It was this background that Paul directed his letter, to confront the false beliefs, and define the teachings of Christ, on some specific matters that still affect us today.

148

A great riot at Ephesus prompted Paul to leave there and return to Corinth. On his way, while in Macedonia, Paul met Titus returning from Corinth, who reported to Paul that his first letter had accomplished much good, but that there were some of the leaders in the Corinthian church who openly rejected Paul as a genuine apostle of Christ. This triggered Paul's second letter to the Corinthians, which he sent ahead with Titus.

The primary purpose of his second letter appears to be Paul's vindication of himself as an apostle of Christ, and to remind the Corinthians that, even though he (Paul) had founded the church there, he did not have the right in its management.

The Book Of Galatians...

Paul's letter to the church at Galatia addressed similar concerns as those in Rome. In this letter, Paul also clarifies that certain acts within the old Jewish Law (including circumcision) were not a part of the gospel of Christ, and had nothing whatever to do with God's salvation.

Paul's work in Galatia had been extremely successful. Great multitudes, mostly Gentiles, had eagerly accepted Christ. But, after Paul's leaving there, Jewish teachers insisted that the Gentiles could not be Christians without keeping the Law of Moses. The Galatians heeded the Jewish counselors with the same passion they had in receiving Paul's message, creating an epidemic of circumcision among the Gentile Christians.

149

There was a sect of early Jewish Christians, known as Judaizers, who were not willing to accept the Apostles' teaching, to insist that all Christians must come to God through Judaism, where circumcision was the inaugural act. To them, in order for a Gentile to be a Christian, they must first become a Jewish proselyte and keep the Jewish law. These Judaizers made it their business to visit and unsettle the Gentile churches, their intention being to stamp Christ with the Jewish trademark.

Paul stood adamant against the Judaizers' movement, knowing that observance to Jewish Law could not be imposed upon the Gentile converts. The expansion and separation of Christianity from the Jewish religion (to embrace the world) was Paul's consuming mission. The effort to Judaize the Gentile churches ended at the fall of Jerusalem in 70 AD, an event that severed all relations between Judaism and Christianity. Up until then Christianity was regarded as a branch of Judaism, but from that time on, the Jews and Christians have been separated both theologically and politically.

Paul spent his life teaching Gentiles that they could be Christians without becoming Jewish proselytes. This is also an important lesson for today...that, being a Christian does not require an allegiance to some organized religion, including the religion of Christianity. The religion of a true Christian is one of devotion to the person of Christ...not to an organization of man.

The Book Of Ephesians...

The New Testament message, revealed in all of Paul's letters, is that God's true church includes every person who has been saved from their sin through God's grace of salvation, as offered by the sacrifice of Jesus, the Christ. That church includes born-again Jews and Gentiles alike.

Membership in the Church of God comes not by the observance of religious laws (Jewish or otherwise). The Mosaic Law and animal (lamb) sacrifices of the Old Testament were God's preparation for the true Lamb of God (Jesus, the Christ). The Old Testament rituals were "types and shadows" of a more certain salvation in the form of a more certain sacrifice.

This message of God's inspired apostle (Paul) displeased the Jews greatly. They believed the Mosaic Law was binding on everyone, and they were angrily resentful toward uncircumcised Gentiles who called themselves disciples of the Jewish Messiah.

Although Paul taught the Gentile Christians to stand firm in their religious liberty from Jewish law, he did not want them to be biased against their Jewish fellow-Christians, but rather to regard them as brothers and sisters in Christ.

Paul's letter to the Ephesians was written to the leading center of Gentile converts. In it, Paul exalted the oneness, the universality, and the unspeakable glory of the "Body of Christ", another term for the Church of God.

151

The Book Of Philippians...

     Paul's letter to the Christians at Philippi is a missionary letter dealing with a number of things. As a rule, Paul did not accept pay for his preaching, preferring instead to meet his personal needs by working at his trade as a tent maker. There was an occasion, however, when he received an offering from one of the churches in support of his foreign missionary work.

     Three years after his visit to Philippi, while imprisoned in Rome, Paul received a visit from Epaphroditus with an offering. Deeply moved, Paul sent Epaphroditus back to Philippi with an encouraging letter discussing the heavenly goal for the believer and the joy that Paul had in serving Christ. It is a strong letter of hope and comfort with the predominant theme being... "There is joy in the Lord".

     The powerful testimony of this letter can't go unnoticed. It was written by a man in prison who (for thirty years) had been mobbed, beaten and stoned for his preaching...yet here he is, sharing an overflowing joy in serving the Lord. What causes a person to endure such torture when he could have recanted and denied Jesus to save himself? The answer is obvious. Paul knew beyond doubt that Jesus was the resurrected Christ who now rules and intercedes at God's right hand. He knew that Jesus is the answer to all our human problems...and Paul was willing to sacrifice himself for the good news. And he's not alone!

Paul had no other option than to do the ministry God had called him to do. In fulfilling God's will for his life, Paul had an inner peace and joy that no outer persecution or life's trouble could destroy. He's not alone...millions of others throughout history have followed in his footsteps. I'm deeply grateful and humbled to be a part of that family of believers...and I look forward to a long chat with Paul someday when he and I are not too busy up there...where the good stuff has replaced the pain and suffering of things down here. Thanks, Paul.

The Book Of Colossians...

Another of Paul's letters, while he was still imprisoned at Rome, was to the people at Colosse. He wrote this letter after hearing about a dangerous heresy that was developing in the local church.

A mixture of Greek, Jewish and Oriental religious ideas had begun to invade the purity of Christ's teachings, confusing some believers. Among other things, the cultish philosophers were calling for the worship of angels as intermediaries between God and man, and were also insisting on a rigorous observance of certain Jewish requirements.

Spiritually untrained and immature Christian believers were being assaulted with pompous expressions as "Christian theology" that were, in reality, promoting cultish beliefs to the confusion of God's true believers. Something had to be done.

153

Paul's letter addressed the problem. He reminded the believers of the deity and power of Christ as the fulfillment for human need...and that no other in the universe is superior to the one God (revealed in Christ) and no other is worthy of worship. Paul's carefully written statements regarding the doctrines of the Gospel were designed for reading aloud in the local church.

The Two Books Of Thessalonians...

The church at Thessalonica was founded on one of Paul's missionary journeys, but he was not privileged to remain there very long to instruct the church. Paul sent a young minister (Timothy) to offer assistance. Timothy sent word to Paul that the Christians in Thessalonica were bravely bearing up under the persecutions that many other Christians were being faced with because of their belief...but that they had some heavy questions.

The faithful believers at Thessalonica were curious about those Christians who had died, wondering how they would get any benefit at the Lord's return to earth. Apparently, Paul had zealously taught of Jesus' second coming while he was there.

To answer their concern, Paul wrote his first letter to inform them that those, who had previously died, would not be left behind when the Lord returns. They will also enjoy the benefits of the general resurrection of all dead Christians. His second letter to the Thessalonica church was written a few weeks or months after the first, to clarify the time of the Lord's return.

154

In his first letter, Paul identifies the Lord's coming as sudden and unexpected, while in the second letter, he clarifies that it will not occur until after the great apostasy has occurred. The book of Revelation deals with this religious apostasy at great length, to reveal the time span of 1260 years, beginning around 270 AD, long after the death of Paul and the other disciples.

The Letters To Timothy And Titus...

Paul's letters to Timothy and Titus are referred to as the "pastoral epistles". Both men traveled with Paul as understudies in his missionary journeys.

In these "pastoral" letters, Paul provides instructions on how they were to minister...dealing with such matters as the emergence of false teachers within the churches, women's place in the church, bishops and deacons, widows and elders...and about the role of a true minister.

In his last letter to Timothy, Paul shares his final words and his triumphant shout of faith in Christ...just before he was beheaded for his Christian testimony.

The Book Of Hebrews...

The book of Romans was written for the Gentiles. The book of Hebrews was written for the Jewish mind. In this letter, Paul defines the relationship of the New Testament Christ to the Levitical priesthood and temple sacrifices of the Old Testament. The Hebrew book brings the Old and New Testaments into one.

Even after accepting Jesus as their personal Savior, many Jewish Christians continued to observe the temple rituals and sacrifices taught in the Old Testament. Most Jews believed that their beloved city, Jerusalem, would become the world's capital under their Messiah's sovereignty. Instead, their city and temple were totally destroyed (70 AD) by the Romans, bringing the Jewish temple rituals and sacrifices to an end.

The book of Hebrews explains that animal sacrifices and temple rituals are no longer necessary...that they were intended to be expressions of faith in looking forward to a future Messiah, who would shed His blood as the ultimate sacrifice for the sins of mankind. In short, the book of Hebrews turns our attention away from religious rituals and toward the blood of Jesus as the answer for our sinful rebellion against our Creator.

The Book Of James...

James, an apostle of Jesus, was inspired to share some practical guidelines for Christian believers, to help them in their faith and conduct. James talks of wisdom, good works and pure religion...as well as issues like patience, faith, temptation, and respect of others. Filled with moral precepts, the book of James defines down-to-earth Christian ethical standards.

While Paul's writings confront our Christian faith with doctrinal understanding, James looks at Christian faith through conduct, to resolve the relationship of faith and good works.

156

The Two Books Of Peter...

The apostle, Peter, directed his letters to the persecuted churches in Asia Minor (founded by Paul). At the time of these letters (around 66 AD), the gospel of Christ had already spread throughout the Roman Empire, luring masses of converts from the pagan Roman religions to Christianity.

Urged on by leaders of the threatened pagan religions, the Roman government applied its political and military power against the Christians. At the time of Peter's writing the church was suffering some of its greatest trials of persecution under Nero. The Roman government had falsely accused the Christians of a terrible crime to justify their harsh, cruel punishment.

Peter wrote his first letter shortly after Paul's martyrdom (and just before his own) to encourage other believers to bear up under their sufferings. In an atmosphere of great persecution, Peter exhorted Christians not to think it strange that they suffered for their faith, reminding them that Christ likewise suffered. He also reminded the believers of the glorious inheritance with God that awaited them when this life is over...reassuring them that their earthly pilgrimage is momentary, and secondary, to the eternal life that waits beyond. This reality has been the strength of every Christian in every generation...that no earthly trouble or persecution can defeat our relationship with God...nor destroys the eternal reward awaiting those who remain faithful to Christ.

157

In his second letter, Peter predicts the coming apostasy of the "Christian religion", just as Paul had done in his letters. Peter's message to the true church is…that we make certain that the hope of our salvation is by faith in Christ alone…and not by faith in religion.

The Books Of John…

The three epistles (letters) written by the apostle, John, emphasize the main focus of the Gospel, warning believers of the heresies that would later produce a corrupt and pagan form of Christianity. John emphasized the fact that Jesus is the righteous Son of God, and those who follow him must live righteously in an unrighteous world…and that to fulfill the will of God is to love one another. John's second and third letters cautioned against false teachers.

The Book Of Jude…

Jude, a brother of Jesus, further warns of the coming religious apostasy, encouraging believers of every generation to maintain the true faith delivered to the true saints of God (those born-again believers known as the "Church of God").

The Book Of Revelation…

The grand finale of the Bible story is the prophecy book entitled "The Revelation Of Jesus Christ" to reveal events that would take place during the "Christian era".

The "Christian era" encompasses the earthly life of the true Christian church...beginning at the death and resurrection of Christ (33 AD) and continuing until a future date, when Jesus returns to earth to redeem his church and deliver it to God and its heavenly reward.

The Revelation visions are symbolic portrayals of real events that would occur during the Christian era. The fact that these events have occurred precisely as the Revelation said they would is a powerful evidence to the Bible's prophetical ability.

There are confusing and conflicting interpretations of the Revelation's message, although it isn't confusing, at all, to the sincere Bible student. The Revelation can easily and correctly be interpreted, but this is a topic we will take up in another writing.

CONCLUDING THOUGHTS

There is no greater wisdom to be found anywhere on earth than what is revealed to us in the Bible's New Testament.

Everyone who has studied it with an open mind and pure intent for truth has come away with the same respect and awe that millions of other readers have found before them. Only a omniscient God could have designed and taught such wisdom. The greatest undertaking in life is to learn and follow God's eternal precepts...and with sincere prayer, you and I are assured to succeed. Everywhere we look, reality just keeps getting better and better.

The Life, The Person The Teachings Of Jesus, The Christ

Throughout history there have been many teachers and prophets who spoke of urgent and important issues. Some of those teachers and prophets were sent from God and their words have been captured for us in the Old Testament. But, in all of human history, there has never been a greater prophet or teacher than Jesus Christ. His message and authority are unparalleled.

Throughout his life Jesus declared that he was the only begotten Son of God...the promised Messiah (Christ). Every person who has thoroughly researched his life with an open mind has come to the same conclusion.

Jesus' sermon on the mount (Matthew chapters 5,6) and his final message (John chapters 14,15,16) have been heralded throughout the world as the most profound pieces of literature ever recorded. They provide insights that are found nowhere else in human writing. And after centuries of scientific progress and social change, the teachings of Jesus remain so relevant to our human life that they could have been written exclusively for our generation alone. The continuing wisdom and relevance of Jesus' teachings about life, health and happiness is truly miraculous.

160

God's wisdom alone, as revealed to us through His Son, could endure time to remain relevant. God understands human beings as no one else can. He knows our needs, our pain, our suffering, our ambitions, our problems...and the solutions to all our troubles. His son, Jesus, has given wisdom to the human race that can be found nowhere else. It is a wise person who seeks to understand the teachings of the eternally wise Jesus.

Throughout Old Testament history, God called several men as His prophets, to declare God's message. These prophets knew that they were only forerunners of God's "true prophet", who would eventually arrive on earth to reveal God as no other person could do. Jesus was that true prophet.

The masses of people, who heard him teach, recognized Jesus as God's special prophet. His message, his miracles and his pure life confirmed his Divine mission.

"But when they sought to lay hands on him (Jesus), they feared the multitude, because they took him for a prophet."

Matthew 21:46

"And there came a fear on all: and they glorified God, saying, that a great prophet is risen up among us; and, That God hath visited his people."   Luke 7:16

"Then those men, when they had seen the miracle that Jesus did, said, this is of a truth that prophet that should come into the world."   John 6:14

The Message of Jesus...

The message of Jesus is simple, straightforward and effective. It can be summarized in one word..."love". For those who learn to follow its guidelines (love God, love yourself, love other human beings) the results are a happy, peaceful, successful and stable life. What more can a person want?

Jesus introduced us to a loving Heavenly Father (our Creator) who desires the very best for every human being on earth. Throughout his life and ministry Jesus showed us the power of what love could do. He also defined love as the one single commandment that satisfies God's will for our life...

> (Words of Jesus) "Thou shalt love the Lord thy God with all thy heart, and with all thy soul, and with all thy mind. This is the first and great commandment. And the second is like unto it, Thou shalt love thy neighbor as thyself. On these two commandments hang all the law and the prophets."
>
> Matthew 22:37-40

The Authority of Jesus' Message...

Those who were privileged to hear Jesus speak realized the authority and wisdom of his teachings. Never had anyone spoken with such power and insight. There was something unique about this messenger, who taught of things far beyond the wisdom and training of mere mortals. His words remain today as the most influential and effective guidelines for human life.

THE EXISTENCE OF JESUS
PRIOR TO HIS EARTHLY VISIT

The Bible is emphatically clear in announcing the eternal divinity of Jesus…that the existence of Jesus <u>did not begin</u> at a baby's birth some 2000 years ago in Bethlehem.

"In the beginning was the Word, and the Word was with God, and the Word was God. The same was in the beginning with God. All things were made by him; and without him was not any thing made that was made. And the Word was made flesh, and dwelt among us, (and we beheld his glory, the glory as of the only begotten of the Father,) full of grace and truth. John (the Baptist) bare witness of him, and cried, saying, This was he of whom I spake, He that cometh after me is preferred before me: for he was before me. And of his fulness have all we received, and grace for grace. No man hath seen God at any time; the only begotten Son, which is in the bosom of the Father, he hath declared him." John 1:1-3, 14-18

"Jesus said, "Your father Abraham rejoiced to see my day: and he saw it, and was glad." Then said the Jews unto him, "Thou art not yet fifty years old, and hast thou seen Abraham?" Jesus said unto them, "Verily, verily, I say unto you, Before Abraham was, I am."   John 8:56-58

(Jesus' prayer)"And now, O Father, glorify thou me with thine own self with the glory which I had with thee before the world was."   John 17:5

163

THE EXISTENCE OF JESUS
DURING HIS EARTHLY VISIT

This is the part of Jesus' existence most familiar to us, since it is the part taught at length in the scriptures. The eight segments of his earthly life are...(1) Old Testament prophecies (2) birth and youth (3) temptations (4) ministry (5) teachings (6) persecution and suffering (7) death (8) resurrection.

Fulfilled Prophesies Regarding Jesus' Life...

The numerous Old Testament prophecies of the coming Messiah revealed his life and ministry in such detail that it would be impossible to mistake the real Messiah when he arrived.

The human lineage, manner of birth, place of birth, exact year of birth, his ministry, his betrayal, his trial, method of death, and his resurrection were prophesied centuries before Messiah was born.

The historical Jesus of Nazareth (who we read about in the Bible) has fulfilled every single one of the Old Testament prophecies as they were foretold...in perfect detail.

The Birth and Youth of Jesus...

The Bible provides extensive details regarding the birth of Jesus but there is little known of His growing years other than one event when He was twelve years old...when he amazed the religious leaders in the temple with his spiritual insights.

The Temptation of Jesus...

God cannot be tempted with evil...nor does He tempt human beings with evil. Yet, humans are constantly tempted to rebel against God and His laws. This human situation is one that God was not exposed to, until He took on the flesh of a human being. As a result, God now understands our human dilemma and is able to sympathize with and help those who come to Him for deliverance from temptation. God realizes how weak we are within our human flesh to combat the evil temptations of Satan ...that we weak human beings need divine help.

Human temptations are divided into three areas...(1) lust of the flesh (2) lust of the eye (3) pride of life (I John 2:16). Jesus, the incarnate God, was exposed to these three temptations prior to entering His public ministry...and he defeated Satan in the flesh and in the Spirit.

Because Jesus is a victor over temptation, and because he is our strength, we too can be victorious. Here are a couple Bible references to put this all in perspective...

"Let no man say when he is tempted, I am tempted of God: for God cannot be tempted with evil, neither tempts he any man."   James 1:13

"For all that is in the world, the lust of the flesh, and the lust of the eyes, and the pride of life, is not of the Father, but is of the world."   1 John 2:16

165

" Then was Jesus led up of the Spirit into the wilderness to be tempted of the devil. And when he had fasted forty days and forty nights, he was afterward an hungered. And when the tempter came to him, he said, If thou be the Son of God, command that these stones be made bread (*lust of the flesh*). But he answered and said, It is written, Man shall not live by bread alone, but by every word that proceedeth out of the mouth of God. Then the devil taketh him up into the holy city, and setteth him on a pinnacle of the temple, And saith unto him, If thou be the Son of God, cast thyself down: for it is written, He shall give his angels charge concerning thee: and in their hands they shall bear thee up, lest at any time thou dash thy foot against a stone (*pride of life*). Jesus said unto him, It is written again, Thou shalt not tempt the Lord thy God. Again, the devil taketh him up into an exceeding high mountain, and showeth him all the kingdoms of the world, and the glory of them; and saith unto him, All these things will I give thee, if thou wilt fall down and worship me (*lust of the eye*). Then saith Jesus unto him, Get thee hence, Satan: for it is written, Thou shalt worship the Lord thy God, and him only shalt thou serve. Then the devil leaveth him, and, behold, angels came and ministered unto him."

Matthew 4:1-11

"Seeing then that we have a great high priest, that is passed into the heavens, Jesus the Son of God, let us hold fast our profession. For we have not an high priest which cannot be touched with the feeling of our infirmities; but was in all points tempted like as we are, yet without sin. Let us therefore come boldly unto the throne of grace, that we may obtain mercy, and find grace to help in time of need."

Hebrews 4:14-16

166

The Earthly Ministry of Jesus...

The ministry of Jesus consisted of his teachings and his healing miracles...both of which are well documented in the Bible. John revealed, however, that the earthly ministry of Jesus was so extensive that it was not possible for the Gospel writers to record everything...

> "And there are also many other things which Jesus did, the which, if they should be written every one, I suppose that even the world itself could not contain the books that should be written."   John 21:25

The four Gospels provide a detailed record of thirty-five miracles that Jesus performed. Some tell of miraculous events with nature, such as the draught of fishes, stilling the storm, and walking on the water. Others tell of miraculous healings of the blind, the deaf and dumb, leprosy and various other diseases. Also recorded are the casting out of demons and the raising of the dead. On several occasions it is reported that multitudes of people brought their sick and afflicted to Jesus, who *"healed every manner of disease and sickness"*...although a detail of each one of these miracles was not recorded.

The miracles of Jesus were witnessed by huge numbers of people that continued to grow as the word was spread of all that Jesus was doing. Some believed and some didn't.

Many accepted that Jesus was more than just a human being, acknowledging him as God on earth who is capable of all things. Others regarded his miracles as a gift from God to fulfill his role as the prophet. One skeptical religious leader, observing Jesus' ministry, was forced to confront Jesus with a surprising confession ...

"...We know that thou art a teacher come from God: for no man can do these miracles that thou doest, except God be with him."   John 3:2

Even the skeptics of Jesus' day realized that there was something remarkably different about Jesus and his teachings. His disciples also believed...to record 661 Bible references that describe the miracles of Jesus in his three-year earthly ministry. Even so, John reminded us...a library of books could not tell all the things Jesus did while on earth.

Some people question whether this all happened, or if it isn't just a Biblical myth. But you and I can be assured...all the evidence collected over the last 2000 years has totally confirmed the life of Jesus to be just the way the Bible has portrayed it.

Jesus did things that no mere human was capable of doing. He raised the dead, healed every kind of incurable disease and blindness, walked on water, caused the storms to cease, cast out devils...and did many other things that showed his authority over the physical universe...as only God would have.

The Teachings Of Jesus...

The teachings of Jesus are so profound and timely that they could literally change our entire world if they were honored and followed. There is no greater wisdom to be found anywhere on earth than what Jesus taught. Both secular and religious scholars throughout history have referred to his wisdom in their studies and teaching.

Jesus knew the need of our human family, as well as our problems...and He knew the solutions. Those who follow His teachings are enjoying a full and meaningful existence, even in the complex world in which we live. Jesus' teachings touch every important and urgent area of human life. You and I need to look nowhere else to find life's true meaning, purpose and fulfillment. The results are success, happiness, peace, joy, stability and hope ...for anyone who follows the basic truths of Jesus

The two most in-depth recorded lessons of Jesus are His "Sermon On The Mount" (Matthew, chapters 5,6,7) and his "Final Address To His Followers" (John, chapters 14,15,16). Scholars regard the wisdom and timeliness of these two sermons as the "greatest published literature" in all the human writings throughout history. The wisdom of Jesus is heralded throughout the world as far exceeding that of all other teachers...

"He taught them as one having authority, and not as the scribes."   Matthew 7:29

169

Jesus' Teaching To The Religious Leaders...

Jesus went where the religious leaders assembled (in the synagogues) where he was given audience. As they listened to him speak, they were overwhelmed by his truth. Some became jealous and rebelled against Jesus' teaching, while others were humbled and encouraged...embracing the insights and wisdom that only God's true Prophet could possess.

"And Jesus went about all Galilee, teaching in their synagogues, and preaching the gospel of the kingdom, and healing all manner of sickness and all manner of disease among the people."   Matthew 4:23

Jesus' Teaching Ministry To His disciples...

Jesus selected a small group of men as disciples to carry on his message after his return to heaven...often meeting with them privately to further explain his truths to them. During these private meetings, the disciples had the unique privilege of being personally tutored by the God of the universe. Jesus rehearsed his eternal message until their weak human intellect was made to understand his Divine wisdom. These simple and ordinary men became God's ordained scribes to the remaining generations.

"And seeing the multitudes, he went up into a mountain: and when he was set, his disciples came unto him."   Matthew 5:1

170

Jesus' Teaching Ministry To The Masses...

Throughout his public ministry, Jesus made sure that the masses of ordinary people would hear the truths of God. This has been God's divine will throughout history...that every person of every ethnic and cultural background, be made aware of the full will of God for his or her life. The Gospel of Christ is not for a special interest group. Every person on earth is special to God and His truths are available for anyone who desires to know what God is saying to them.

> "And it came to pass, when Jesus had made an end of commanding his twelve disciples, he departed thence to teach and to preach in their cities."   Matthew 11:1

> "And he began again to teach by the sea side: and there was gathered unto him a great multitude, so that he entered into a ship, and sat in the sea; and the whole multitude was by the sea on the land. And he taught them many things by parables, and said unto them in his doctrine..."   Mark 4:1-2

The Method Of Jesus' Teaching...

Jesus often used parables (a picture or story) to illustrate a spiritual truth. His intention is that you and I clearly understand his eternal truth with the promise that, *"you shall know the truth and truth shall set you free"*. I've found that promise to be true.

171

Parables Of Jesus...

The wise and foolish builders	Matthew 7:24-27 Luke 6:47-49
Two debtors	Luke 7:41-47
The rich fool	Luke 12:16-21
The waiting servants	Luke 12:35-40
Barren fig tree	Luke 13:6-9
The sower	Matthew 13:3-23 Mark 4:1-20 Luke 8:5-15
The tares	Matthew 13:24-43
Seed growing secretly	Mark 4:26-29
Mustard seed	Matthew 13:31-32 Mark 4:30-32 Luke 13:18-19
Leaven	Matthew 13:33 Luke 13:20-21
Hidden treasure	Matthew 13:44
Pearl of great price	Matthew 13:45-46
Draw net	Matthew 13:47-50
Unmerciful servant	Matthew 18:23-35
Good Samaritan	Luke 10:30-37
Friend at midnight	Luke 11:5-8
Good shepherd	John 10:1-16
Great supper	Luke 14:15-24
Lost sheep	Matthew 18:12-14 Luke 15:3-7
Lost piece of money	Luke 15:8-10

The prodigal and his brother	Luke 15:11-32
The unjust steward	Luke 16:1-9
Rich man and Lazarus	Luke 16:19-31
Importunate widow	Luke 18:1-8
Pharisee and publican	Luke 18:9-14
Laborers in the vineyard	Matthew 20:1-16
The pounds	Luke 19:11-27
The two sons	Matthew 21:28-32
Wicked husbandmen	Matt 21:33-44 Mark 12:1-12 Luke 20:9-18
Marriage of the king's son	Matthew 22:1-14
Fig tree leafing	Matthew 24:32 Mark 13:28-29
Man taking a far journey	Mark 13:34-37
Ten virgins	Matthew 25:1-13
Talents	Matthew 25:14-30
The vine	John 15:1-5

"And the disciples came, and said unto him, Why speakest thou unto them in parables? He answered and said unto them, Because it is given unto you to know the mysteries of the kingdom of heaven, but to them it is not given. For whosoever hath, to him shall be given, and he shall have more abundance: but whosoever hath not, from him shall be taken away even that he hath. Therefore speak I to them in parables: because they seeing see not; and hearing they hear not, neither do they understand."   Matthew 13:10-13

The Prophecies Of Jesus...

During his earthly ministry Jesus prophesied of future events so precisely that they continue to amaze scholars even today. Their fulfillment is certain proof of his Godly status.

The most famous of his prophecies is the one regarding the destruction of Jerusalem (Matthew 24:1-22; Luke 21:6-24). Standing in front of the temple, Jesus announced to his followers that the Roman Gentiles would destroy the city and temple. He made this prophecy at a time of world peace. There were no uprisings or wars anywhere in the world. The Jews were enjoying peace with the Romans without any threat to their land or religious freedom. Why then would Jesus make such a prophecy? From where did He get His information?

Jesus described the destruction of Jerusalem as, "*a great tribulation such as the world has never seen*". Thirty-seven years after his death, this prophecy came true precisely the way Jesus had warned. Titus, the Roman general, led his army's attack upon Jerusalem with the force and animosity of animals...killing and persecuting the Jewish people, so violently, that today's war lords shake their heads at the merciless brutality of the Romans. Never in all the chronicles of war has there been such cruelty displayed on a people as was done by Titus on the Jews at Jerusalem in 70 AD. How did Jesus know it would happen? He knew...because Jesus was God who knows all things.

Jesus went on to reveal a time when the Jews would once again take control of Jerusalem as their capital. He was looking far into the future, to the year 1967 AD, to prophesy an event that was highly unlikely and virtually impossible...yet it happened just the way Jesus said it would. And there are other prophecies of Jesus that continue to be fulfilled at this very moment. His wisdom in understanding future events strongly supports the claim of Jesus...that he is, indeed, God incarnate in human flesh.

The Sufferings and Persecution Of Jesus...

Why was Jesus ridiculed, persecuted and put to death? Was he a threat to overthrow the Roman government? No! Was he a criminal? No! Did He preach and teach evil doctrines against the Jewish faith? No!

All Jesus did was to preach love and heal people. All Jesus did was to give hope to the downtrodden. All Jesus did was to do good works and to respect our human family. Even so, they mocked him, persecuted him and then killed him. Why?

It was prophesied before he was born that it all would happen. But why did heaven allow Jesus to be punished and persecuted? Why didn't the legions of angels, who were waiting his command, deliver Jesus from the hands of evil men? Why did the God of creation hang on a cross? The answer is love.

"And as Moses lifted up the serpent in the wilderness, even so must the Son of man be lifted up: That whosoever believeth in him should not perish, but have eternal life. For God so loved the world, that he gave his only begotten Son, that whosoever believeth in him should not perish, but have everlasting life. For God sent not his Son into the world to condemn the world; but that the world through him might be saved. He that believeth on him is not condemned: but he that believeth not is condemned already, because he hath not believed in the name of the only begotten Son of God. And this is the condemnation, that light is come into the world, and men loved darkness rather than light, because their deeds were evil. For every one that doeth evil hateth the light, neither cometh to the light, lest his deeds should be reproved. But he that doeth truth cometh to the light, that his deeds may be made manifest, that they are wrought in God."   John 3:14-21

"Then the soldiers of the governor took Jesus into the common hall, and gathered unto him the whole band of soldiers. And they stripped him, and put on him a scarlet robe. And when they had platted a crown of thorns, they put it upon his head, and a reed in his right hand: and they bowed the knee before him, and mocked him, saying, "Hail, King of the Jews!" And they spit upon him, and took the reed, and smote him on the head. And after that they had mocked him, they took the robe off from him, and put his own raiment on him, and led him away to crucify him."   Matthew 27:27-31

"He is despised and rejected of men; a man of sorrows, and acquainted with grief: and we hid as it were our faces from him; he was despised, and we esteemed him not. Surely he hath borne our griefs, and carried our sorrows: yet we did esteem him stricken, smitten of God, and afflicted. But he was wounded for our transgressions, he was bruised for our iniquities: the chastisement of our peace was upon him; and with his stripes we are healed. He was oppressed, and he was afflicted, yet he opened not his mouth: he is brought as a lamb to the slaughter, and as a sheep before her shearers is dumb, so he openeth not his mouth...and he made his grave with the wicked, and with the rich in his death; because he had done no violence, neither was any deceit in his mouth. Yet it pleased the Lord to bruise him; he hath put him to grief: when thou shalt make his soul an offering for sin, he shall see his seed, he shall prolong his days, and the pleasure of the LORD shall prosper in his hand."   Isaiah 53:3-10

God has loved us so much that he provided a supreme sacrifice in the person of His son...Jesus, the Christ...who knew his role as God's sacrificial lamb and willingly endured the anger and arrogance of men who thought themselves more powerful than God. Jesus did what he did, so that you and I could be restored to the fellowship of our Creator and find eternal life.

The tragedy of Jesus' sufferings is that there are those who still reject the greatest love the world has ever known.

The Death of Jesus...

The life and death of Jesus are historical facts confirmed by many sources. But what is so remarkable about the life of Jesus, including His death, is that it was all prophesied centuries before, including dates and situations that only God could have known beforehand. For example, the amazing prophecy about the method by which Jesus was crucified (described by Isaiah seven hundred years previously) was a method of death not yet invented in Isaiah' time. God not only revealed that the Messiah would be crucified at a certain future date...He also described the manner of crucifixion which had not yet been conceived by evil men.

And just as remarkable is the Old Testament prophecy that revealed the exact date when Jesus would be crucified. There is no question of the true identify of God's Messiah...

" Know therefore and understand, that from the going forth of the commandment to restore and to build Jerusalem unto the Messiah the Prince shall be seven weeks, and threescore and two weeks: the street shall be built again, and the wall, even in troublous times. And after threescore and two weeks shall Messiah be cut off, but not for himself: and the people of the prince that shall come shall destroy the city and the sanctuary; and the end thereof shall be with a flood, and unto the end of the war desolations are determined."   Daniel 9:25-26 (words of Jesus) "Therefore doth my Father love me, because I lay down my life, that I might take it again. No man taketh it from me, but I lay it down of myself. I have power to lay it down, and I have power to take it again. This commandment have I received of my Father."   John 10:17-18

The Resurrection of Jesus...

The question for some people is, "Did the resurrection of Jesus really happen ?" The answer is...beyond doubt!

The evidence is overwhelming that Jesus did, indeed, resurrect from the dead...just as he said he would. In another writing we deal with the evidence at length. For those who have taken the time to do the research, there is no doubt.

The political and religious authorities of Jesus' day had a serious problem on their hands when Jesus returned to life three days after He was crucified. The masses of people were now convinced that Jesus was telling the truth and that their Messiah had been wrongly judged and crucified. To cover up their crime, the politicians and priests conspired to concoct a false story... that Jesus' disciples had stolen his body from the tomb. Their story had many loopholes and was never accepted by the people.

If the Roman guards, who were assigned to guard the tomb of Jesus, had fallen asleep at their post...they would have automatically been put to death by their superiors as punishment ...but no guard was ever punished.

179

If they had fallen asleep, how could a few men have rolled away the huge stone that covered the grave entrance, so quietly as not to disturb one single guard lying next to the grave asleep? If the disciples had actually been successful in doing this why was there never an all out search and investigation by the Roman and Jewish officials to make certain to recover the body of Jesus? Why was not one disciple brought before the court to confess what they did with the body?

Instead of being brought before any investigators, after the body was discovered to be missing, the disciples were left alone, as they preached everywhere in public places to masses of people...telling them that Jesus had resurrected...while the religious and political leaders helplessly looked on.

If the disciples had stolen and hidden the body of Jesus, why was there never anyone of the masses of followers to betray their hoax by revealing it to the authorities?

If the disciples had stolen the body of Jesus...where in the world would they have hidden it so that it would never be recovered? Would not this still be the number one priority of every other religion on earth...to uncover the body of Jesus to prove that He was a hoax...if they really believed He was?

If the disciples had stolen and hidden the body of Jesus, to cover up a hoax started by a now dead man...why would they suffer imprisonment, beatings and death for a lie?

How could the disciples have turned something over that they didn't have, and how could they not have gone out into the world to tell others about the most remarkable event that has ever occurred in all of human history?

The disciples died for their teaching because they knew the truth...Jesus was alive. They had seen him, conversed with him and were being empowered by his Spirit to preach those things they knew for certain were true. Physical punishment and death were a small price to pay for the privilege of sharing the message of a living Savior to the world.

(Words of Jesus) "For as Jonas was three days and three nights in the whale's belly; so shall the Son of man be three days and three nights in the heart of the earth."   Matthew 12:40

" To whom (apostles) also he (Jesus) showed himself alive after his passion (resurrection) by many infallible proofs, being seen of them forty days, and speaking of the things pertaining to the kingdom of God."   Acts 1:3

"And when they had fulfilled all that was written of him, they took him down from the tree, and laid him in a sepulchre. But God raised him from the dead: And he was seen many days of them which came up with him from Galilee to Jerusalem, who are his witnesses unto the people."   Acts 13:29-31

181

The Existence of Jesus Today...

Two thousand years ago, a man named Jesus walked on the earth, healing all manner of disease and teaching powerful truths of hope for our human family. The religious and political leaders killed him, not because he was a threat...but because he loved like no one ever loved. Three days after His crucifixion, Jesus resurrected from the dead. Where is He now?

"Jesus said unto them, 'Thus it is written, and thus it behoved Christ to suffer, and to rise from the dead the third day: And that repentance and remission of sins should be preached in his name among all nations, beginning at Jerusalem. And ye are witnesses of these things. And, behold, I send the promise of my Father upon you: but tarry ye in the city of Jerusalem, until ye be endued with power from on high." And he led them out as far as to Bethany, and he lifted up his hands, and blessed them. And it came to pass, while he blessed them, he was parted from them, and carried up into heaven. And they worshipped him, and returned to Jerusalem with great joy: And were continually in the temple, praising and blessing God."
                                                            Luke 24:46-53

(Words of Jesus) "In my Father's house are many mansions: if it were not so, I would have told you. I go to prepare a place for you. And if I go and prepare a place for you, I will come again, and receive you unto myself; that where I am, there ye may be also."
                                                            John 14:2-3

"And when he (Jesus) had spoken these things, while they beheld, he was taken up; and a cloud received him out of their sight. And while they looked stedfastly toward heaven as he went up, behold, two men stood by them in white apparel; Which also said, Ye men of Galilee, why stand ye gazing up into heaven? This same Jesus, which is taken up from you into heaven, shall so come in like manner as ye have seen him go into heaven."   Acts 1:9-11

"So then after the Lord had spoken unto them, he was received up into heaven, and sat on the right hand of God." Mark 16:19

"Therefore being by the right hand of God exalted, and having received of the Father the promise of the Holy Ghost, he hath shed forth this, which ye now see and hear."   Acts 2:33

"And what is the exceeding greatness of God's power to usward who believe, according to the working of his mighty power, Which he wrought in Christ, when he raised him from the dead, and set him at his own right hand in the heavenly places, Far above all principality, and power, and might, and dominion, and every name that is named, not only in this world, but also in that which is to come: And hath put all things under his feet, and gave him to be the head over all things to the church, Which is his body, the fulness of him that filleth all in all."   Ephesians 1:19-23

"Wherefore God also hath highly exalted him (Jesus), and given him a name which is above every name: That at the name of Jesus every knee should bow, of things in heaven, and things in earth, and things under the earth; And that every tongue should confess that Jesus Christ is Lord, to the glory of God the Father."   Philippians 2:9-11

"Jesus is gone into heaven, and is on the right hand of God; angels and authorities and powers being made subject unto him."   1 Peter 3:22

"Seeing then that we have a great high priest, that is passed into the heavens, Jesus the Son of God, let us hold fast our profession. For we have not an high priest which cannot be touched with the feeling of our infirmities; but was in all points tempted like as we are, yet without sin. Let us therefore come boldly unto the throne of grace, that we may obtain mercy, and find grace to help in time of need."   Hebrews 4:14

This Jesus, who was mocked and crucified with common criminals two thousand years ago, now sits at the right hand of God in the place of highest honor and sovereignty in the universe. His role on earth was finished when he became the sacrifice and savior for the sins of mankind. His now rules as the King over his eternal spiritual kingdom and over his church on earth (born-again believers)...making intercession for anyone who comes to God through Him.

184

The Perfect Example Of Jesus' Life...

The way Jesus lived and the message he taught cannot be compared to any other human being. His life was perfect and pure...the embodiment of all that's right in the world.

Jesus lived and taught without prejudice or personal ambition. His motives and actions were chaste and exemplary. He sought not to become a political, military or religious leader. He did not desire wealth or high social position.

The stimulus for Jesus' life and ministry was love. It was the message he lived by, the message he taught, and the message through which he brought hope and healing to every human being in need. His entire earthly ministry is summarized in the theme..."*Greater love has no man than this...that a man lay down his life for another*".

The love of Christ, his teaching of love, and his supreme non-militant, non-political sacrifice, identify him to be someone beyond the normal motives of human activists. Jesus came to reveal God, and to make a way by which we could be reconciled to God's fellowship, even after we revolted against our Creator.

The Followers of Jesus...

Jesus lived and ministered during the time of the oppressive Roman Empire. Even the Jewish nation, where He ministered, was under Roman rule that allowed the Jewish people their religious rituals as a political convenience.

Whatever was done in Israel was done under the watchful eye of Roman officials...as well as the Jewish religious hierarchy, who had befriended the Roman rulers. The life and message of Jesus was antagonistic to the self-exalted position of those Jewish religious leaders. Had the Jewish leaders accepted Jesus as the Messiah, their position would have been in jeopardy, both with the Jews and with the Romans.

For that reason, the religious leaders did everything in their power to discredit and destroy the life and message of Christ. But even after they convinced the Romans to kill Jesus, the Jewish leadership had to deal with His resurrection and with His followers who continued to preach in His name. Using their political influence with the Romans, the Jewish leaders harassed, imprisoned and put to death those who would not denounce Jesus. But that didn't stop Jesus' followers.

Every one of the original twelve disciples, except John, was murdered for their preaching about Jesus. John's fate was to be put in exile on the island of Patmos, where he lived alone to an advanced old age.

The Jews stoned Stephen to death in a public street for his testimony of Christ. The apostle Paul, who once had been part of the Jewish leadership in trying to destroy the Christians, became a convert himself and was eventually beheaded by the Romans for his preaching of Jesus as the Christ.

186

Even at the expense of personal safety, all the early followers of Christ, who were there when He died, continued to teach everywhere that Jesus was the Messiah who had risen from the dead...even though they were certain of personal suffering.

Throughout the centuries, true followers of Christ have endured imprisonment, cruel and inhumane punishment, and even death at the hands of political powers and religionists...yet they all remained faithful to their allegiance to Christ. Why?

The answer is simple...they all knew beyond a shadow of doubt that Jesus was the promised Christ of God, and they were willing to give their lives so that His message would be advanced. The fact that the early disciples, who were personal witnesses to the life and teachings of Jesus, would give their lives for his cause is a powerful testimony to the credibility of Jesus. No man or woman would die for a known hoax.

The fact that countless numbers of "true" Christians throughout the centuries have suffered and died for the message of Christ is a powerful testimony to the credibility of Jesus. No man or woman would die for a known hoax.

The fact that people today continue to be harassed...and even put to death for their allegiance to Christ...is a powerful testimony to the credibility of Jesus. No man or woman would die for a known hoax. Everywhere we look, reality just keeps getting better and better.

Ready For Some More
Really Great News...?

Hi, it's me again...Ken Howard...the guy who wrote the stuff you've been reading in this little book. I hope you have found me to be upfront and honest with you so far...that I've been trying to pass along some useful information that can help make a positive difference in your life.

As we close this discussion I would like to reveal some personal things about myself to let you know that real humans do experience some miraculous things in their lives that can be credited only to God's kind intervention.

People ask me in counseling sessions and seminars, "Do you really believe in the Bible and do you believe that God is interested enough to become involved in my life?" They were actually asking ..."Do you have any experience to back up your beliefs?" Head knowledge alone doesn't get the job done!

To answer those who may have similar questions I submit the following personal experiences that happened just as they are recorded here. As I share these experiences you should know that I am suspicious of personal reports of "miracles" and "visions"....just as I am sure you are. But I cannot shy away from that which I personally know to be absolutely true.

Do true miracles happen and does God really get involved with the ordinary events of our life? You be the judge from what you are about to read.

The following true experiences are shared as my effort to set on record the evidence that God does intervene in behalf of our human family...and that even in these difficult times in which we live there is Divine help and hope for every situation.

I share these experiences with the hope that they will be an encouragement for you. No one is more special to God than you are...and every need of your life is as much a concern to God as are the needs of every other human being. God is capable, willing and available to help in your most difficult of circumstance. There is no problem without an answer and there is no situation without hope. I know from experience.

My problem is in deciding what experiences to include in this short writing, for I have many events to share. God's interventions throughout my adult life can only be described as remarkable, to say the least...beyond human understanding. I still stand in awe as I bring each one to memory.

I do not regard myself to be distinctly deserving of God's attention beyond others of my human family...for it is my belief that every human being is loved of God and that His resources are available to everyone. The few experiences that I share are not the result of anything I have done to earn them, but rather the results of God's merciful grace in behalf of my need.

I've selected four miracles to share from the long list of miracles that have occurred to me personally. But first, let me define a miracle from God as I understand it to be and how it is used in this writing.

A MIRACLE OF GOD DEFINED

A miracle of God is something that happens without any human intervention...a "special visitation" of God beyond the normal and natural processes of nature, science or human expertise. A miracle is something that God performs in an individual's life that cannot be explained any other way.

A "miracle of God" should be distinguished from other "miracles", in that a special visitation from God takes place in behalf of human need.

Each event you are about to read involved a special visitation from God without any human involvement to supply a special need in my life.

WHERE I'M COMING FROM

Simply stated, I am a human being like other human beings...a person who God loves and who God desires to help. I have a normal family life, I've seen both the good and the bad times and I make mistakes. I have an extensive college education and a professional background. I regard myself to be well educated, stable and clear thinking.

I am identified professionally to be an all disciplines certified researcher, a human behavioral scientist, a private counseling Psychologist, a marriage and family counselor, a corporate employee referral counselor, a law enforcement stress management advisor, a theologian, a student of history, a college professor, a seminar speaker, a husband of one wife, a father of three daughters (all grown)...and I own my own home and cut my own grass.

I also do woodworking as a hobby...and I've been known to take the controls of an airplane, to do a few stalls and spins every now and then. Whew...maybe I should think about retiring (at least from grass cutting)!

I've never been a "religious" person in the context of being a devotee or supporter of any specific religion or denominational group of human origin...including the "religion of Christianity". I've not seen the need in my life to become a member of organized religion.

In other words, I am not a "Protestant" or "Catholic"... nor do I endorse any ancient or eastern religions that are popular with New Age ideologies. I am, however, a believer and follower of Jesus Christ and His teachings.

My faith and allegiance to Christ have been determined by the irrefutable scientific and historical evidence that proves Jesus is indeed the true Messiah from God...as well as by the numerous miracles I have received through Him.

191

I am an average person who has experienced some extraordinary and miraculous events in my life, as I learned to open myself up to the fellowship of God. The events you are about to read are true. I begin with the most powerful of all miracles...a complete change of character that occurred in an instant moment of time.

THE MIRACLE OF A NEW LIFE WITH GOD

I married right out of high school and started college and a family at the same time. My first college major was business. I landed an office job with a major paper manufacturer where I was trained and primed for executive responsibilities. I was in the right place at the right time. One of the company's top executives took me under his wing and I was in a position of unlimited advancement even at a very young age. My responsibilities and paycheck continued to grow. Life was good. We bought our first home, enjoyed the niceties and became involved in community projects. I became a pilot and was considering the purchase of a private airplane. I loved to fly.

I was young, proud and healthy. I had been active in sports throughout my life and continued to play in basketball and baseball leagues. I needed nothing. I was in total control. Things could not have been better. It was then that my life was turned upside down, never again to be the same.

One evening while sitting at home I picked up a Bible that someone had given us and opened it to page one. That simple event started a chain of events that led to the most profound experience I have ever had.

I had never bothered to read the Bible before, so I figured it would be something different to glance through. I attribute my curiosity to the faithfulness of my mother who had seen to it that I attended church and Sunday school as a child.

As I began reading at the beginning it didn't take me long to get to "Cain's wife". Where in the world did Cain get His wife? If Adam and Eve were the only two people on earth and they had only two sons, Cain and Abel, then where did Cain's wife come from? Was she an alien from another planet...or is the Bible accurate? This really confused me.

Days went by and I couldn't get the idea of Cain's wife off my mind. My curiosity was highly exaggerated, something out of character for me. I consulted an expert...my grandmother. This was a mistake (actually a blessing) for this was another link that changed my life forever.

I had known for years that my grandmother possessed a special gift of faith and that she was well educated on the Bible. The lady simply knew how to pray to get her prayers answered.

My phone call triggered my grandmother's brain that I was showing an interest in "spiritual" matters. No I wasn't! I just wanted to know where Cain's wife came from.

My life was in good shape and I was very busy. God wasn't important to me. I was getting along just fine without God, so I thought. Maybe I had a few faults but I wasn't as bad as some people I knew. I worked hard, supported my family, did my community stuff...yet there was this occasional twinge of guilt that something was missing.

But, all I wanted was to know "where Cain's wife come from?" yet this dear grandmother decided to pray for my spiritual needs...the result being that my life went into total chaos. Life had been good until then but that was to quickly change. All of the sudden, for the first time in my life, I began to feel guilty and fearful of an approaching punishment. I felt dirty, ugly and sinful. The guilt and fear were so intense that I could not sleep or perform my duties.

I began to experience chest pains and shortness of breath. My whole thought was consumed with dying and going to hell. I did not want to die and be eternally punished. I couldn't go to sleep at night for fear I would die. I couldn't function during the day for fear I would die. Flying was no longer a joy for me but I was still required to travel in my work. The fear of death and hell were so great that I was literally drenched in sweat from takeoff to landing. On one occasion I canceled a flight from New York that would have taken me home in a few hours, opting instead to travel all night by train ...because trains don't fall out of the sky to kill people.

I knew I was having a heart attack…that some terrible disease had invaded my body…that I was going to suddenly die. I consulted with a physician for a complete physical exam. It proved how healthy I was, yet the physician recognized my mental condition to prescribe medication. He assumed it to be job or family related stress. I dared not tell him of my desperate fear of death and hell for fear he would think I was a religious basket case.

I became dissatisfied with life, with my job and with my family. Nothing pleased me anymore. Life was lousy. I decided to quit my job to the dismay of my employer. They couldn't imagine a young man giving up the promising career that was inevitable for me. I was being primed for top executive position. My future was assured…but I was still going to die and go to hell. I quit my job, took another, and quit that job also in less than a month. I didn't realize while all this was going on that it was God dealing with me…that He was being merciful to me.

It was at this point in my life that the most profound miracle I have ever experienced took place. It began when my red Ford took on a mind of its own one June Friday morning.

I was driving to a business appointment with that on my mind. Suddenly my red Ford stopped. I found myself sitting in the middle of an empty church parking lot. What happened? I did not drive my car into the parking lot. I did not want to park here. I wanted to go to a business meeting.

I said to myself, "Ken, you are out of your mind. What in the world are you doing? Get this thing started and get to your meeting."   That's when a voice spoke to me..."Get out of the car and go into the church". Remarkably I obeyed and went to the door...but it was locked. I walked all around the church and every door was locked. No one was there that early on a Friday morning. Thinking how ridiculous this was I walked back to the car, but the voice again spoke..."Return to the church and I will open the door for you." I did so and was shocked when the locked door flew open of its own accord.

I walked in and found myself in the rear of the sanctuary of a large church, looking toward the front at the pulpit and altars. This was the first time I had been inside a church in years. The church was empty except for two ministers who were standing at the altar...waiting for me. One of the ministers, who knew my parents and family, looked up as I entered. He recognized me. As I walked toward him I was rehearsing in my mind what I would say as to the reason I was there in church on a Friday morning. As he reached out to shake my hand I broke down and began to weep. I found myself crying out, "Pastor, I need to be saved."...Whatever that meant I did not then know.

With that, he and the other minister and myself knelt down at an altar of prayer where I began to pray that God would be merciful to forgive my sins. I needed no pastoral counseling. I was not looking to join a church or religion. All I wanted was to be free from the burden of guilt and fear that was haunting me day and night. I wanted my life to be better than what it was.

It was then that the most profound miracle I have ever experienced took place. As I prayed, God entered into my life... but how do you explain an experience like that with words?

In just a few moments of time my life was totally changed. My whole character and outlook were instantly converted to see life as God sees it...even though I knew very little about spiritual things. The guilt and fear that I had been carrying around for years immediately vanished. They were replaced with a peace and joy that I had never before experienced and which remains to this day. I felt totally clean and pure for the first time in my life.

The heavy burden that had been my constant companion had been lifted. Life was not only good again...it was great. I had come into the presence of God. I had experienced His love and forgiveness...and His cleansing. I knew that there was no longer anything between my Creator and me, and that I had been accepted into His Kingdom. My entire sinful past had been miraculously forgiven and erased from God's memory.

I later came to realize that what I had experienced on that Friday morning in June was a spiritual surgery performed by God known as being "born again". Sin had miraculously been cut away and had been replaced with the righteousness of God.

I had been released from the evil power that had control of my life and which had caused me to deny and reject God. I no longer felt guilty or dirty or fearful. I felt clean and loved and accepted.

In an instant of time I had become a child of God and was now part of His family, never again to be alone or without hope. I walked out of the church that day a new man. Everything appeared brighter...life, the trees, the flowers... everything.

The first hard evidence that something miraculous had happened was my shirt pocket. That's where a packet of cigarettes always lived. I dropped the pack in the first trash bin I came to and then another miracle happened. Although I had tried unsuccessfully on several occasions to quit my two-pack-a-day habit...from that moment to this I never again had a desire or craving for another cigarette...not even a passing thought. And the same was true with alcohol, which was becoming more than just social drinking on business trips.

But there was much more than that to come. My entire attitude and outlook about life had miraculously changed. The God I had shunned while I pursued my life was now my entire focus. I wanted to become acquainted with Him and to experience His presence. The truths within the Bible began to open up to me as I devoured the reading of it. I was no longer afraid or confused about life and death. The warmth and embrace of God were now my constant companions.

The miracle of my spiritual "rebirth" was far greater and more effective than what any personal resolution could have achieved. It was an instantaneous experience that completely removed all the things that were wrong, to replace them with all the things that were right.

The results are history. That miracle happened 35 years ago to become the beginning of the rest of my life. The joy and peace remain to this day as I continue to enjoy God's continuing presence...where His love and assurance to me, that all is well, is the foundation of my life.

The miracle of that day was the result of a simple, yet sincere prayer. I had reached a point in my life of realizing that my sins were my whole problem, and that my only hope was to seek forgiveness and deliverance from them. God saw my sincerity and heard my prayer. He did the rest...to perform a spiritual miracle that "religion" is incapable of doing.

I soon came to realize that the reason my prayer was heard and my sins forgiven had nothing to do with my ability to change... or that I had any influence with God. I had no ability to change my life nor did I have any influence with God.

I was like every other human being who has ever lived. I had sinned and failed in the eyes of God, and my sins had separated me from Him. I had nothing to offer or to bargain with. I was a sinner whose sins must be punished. But the good news is...no human being, needs to fear the punishment for sin.

Our punishment was taken by another person, who sacrificed Himself so that our sins could be forgiven…if that is what we desire. God's son, Jesus the Christ, died as a sacrifice for our sins…so that our prayers for forgiveness can be heard and our relationship with God restored.

My prayer was heard, my sins forgiven and my life totally changed because of Jesus, who now lives at the right hand of God as our intercessor…our Messiah. God listens and answers our prayers, not for anything we have done, but only because of what Jesus Christ has done for us. Jesus said it this way, "I am the way, the truth and the life…no man comes to the Father but by me."

What I have just told you is true. I'm not the only person whose life has been miraculously changed by the kind and merciful intervention of our Creator. Millions of other people can share a similar story that transformed their life in a miraculous way.

A SPECIAL VISITATION AND MIRACLE
OF PHYSICAL HEALING

I must confess that I am very skeptical of modern-day "faith healers" who preach a wealth and health gospel. But I am not skeptical of God's ability or desire to heal His people…for I have so been healed on several occasions. Many other people have also testified to similar healings where God intervened without the help of medicine or physicians. One of the more serious situations and blessing was the miraculous healing of terminal cancer...yet the healing was only a small part of the real blessing of that experience.

The doctors and laboratory tests had diagnosed me with a terminal cancer of the most serious kind. There was, and still is, no known cure for this specific type of cancer. The only possible hope was surgery to remove the disease, although once it had invaded the blood stream there was no hope even with surgery. We had no other option, surgery was hastily scheduled.

My hospital room was semi-private with an elderly dying man in the other bed. My family and friends had left for the night and the nursing staff had completed my pre-op for next day surgery. Only a small table light had been left on and the door to our room was closed so that I might get some rest from the hallway noise.

I was alone. For the first time since the cancer diagnosis I was alone with my thoughts of what I was dealing with. I began to pray, but my prayer was not for mercy or healing. Although I don't recall the precise wording, I prayed something like this... "Lord, for the first time in my life I face the reality of possible death as the result of this disease. If that be your will, so be it. I am grateful for the life you have given me and whether I live of die, I shall serve you."

Then the miracle happened just as I now describe it. Suddenly the door to my room opened. It was a heavy door with a self-closing hinge that kept it shut unless propped open. As I lay there watching I realized that no one had opened it, but that the door had opened of its own accord.

Then God walked in. God was not in human form nor did I see a physical image, but God's presence was so powerful that I followed Him step-by-step as He walked from the door to the side of my bed.

It is impossible to describe with mere words the presence that had entered my room. I looked up into the presence of God standing by my bed and I felt His arms encircle me. I felt safe and secure, and at total peace.

Although there was no physical form to see, I knew that I was in the presence of God. I saw Him and heard Him speak with my "spiritual eyes and ears". I was not hallucinating or dreaming. I had not been given any drugs or relaxation pills nor was I hooked up to any equipment or IV's. It was just God and me.

I felt His embrace just as a father would embrace a child who needs assurance and comfort. Then I heard Him speak.

God's voice was not audible yet very clear and decisive. I have heard that same voice numerous times throughout my adult life. It is a voice unmistakable, yet indescribable. The words spoken to me were to this effect...

"I have removed the disease that has invaded your body. You are totally healed. You will not die in surgery tomorrow or any other time from this disease." Then He was gone.

Had God told me to get dressed and leave, that there was no longer the need for surgery, I would have done so…for I knew at that moment I was totally healed. But for whatever reason I do not know…I was still to undergo surgery.

Maybe the surgery was for the benefit of the doctors and my family, who were not privileged to this private visitation from God, to confirm my healing for them.

The surgery went as planned. The lab results told the whole story… "Ken, we have some great news. Not only is there no evidence of the cancer spreading, but the previously infected parts are clean as well."

Simply stated, the scars of more than one hundred stitches in my body need not be here. The surgery accomplished nothing other than as evidence that the great Surgeon had already operated the night before.

That experience left me with a wonderful memory of God's love and mercy that I know He extends to all His children. The great blessing for me was not the healing of a terminal cancer, but rather that God would honor me with His presence and personal visit.

There is no greater blessing than to experience a fellowship with God.

I've enjoyed other physical healings from the Lord over the years, as has my wife and our children...and every experience reminds us of our Heavenly Father's love and mercy. We also have been privileged to participate in and witness miraculous physical healing of other people, which cannot be explained in mere human understanding.

BUT, APPARENTLY, GOD IS INTERESTED IN OTHER THINGS BEYOND SAVING SOULS AND HEALING BODIES

Boy, I sure hope this next story doesn't come across as some fanatic with a yarn to spin. It's about the miraculous healing of an old Rambler transmission. Even my own mother didn't want me to tell this story in such a classy book as this...although she knows it really happened just as I'm about to tell you.

For those of you too young to remember...a Rambler was a car...and even way back in 1964 they made cars with automatic transmissions. When I finally bought the old used Rambler years later, that transmission had been shifted a whole, whole bunch of times.

I've learned over the years that God is interested in every area of our life, both minor and major, to help in situations where things appear to be impossible. The healing of a transmission at a time when my family really needed God's help was one of those occasions. That may sound exaggerated or fanatical, but read on, for this miracle of God happened just as I describe it.

It happened while I was in college with only one car for school and work. My family was very young then...a wife, three daughters (one in diapers). We had all sacrificed for me to continue my education, which we felt the Lord wanted me to pursue. I was working on the freight docks at night to pay our living and school expenses. We always had enough to pay the rent and buy groceries but nothing was left to sock back for "emergencies". Those were left to prayer.

One emergency was the old 1964 Rambler. It had an automatic transmission that did what it was supposed to. When you pointed the gearshift to the "D", it drove forward...and when you pointed it to the "R", it reversed. Life was good. Then the unspeakable happened. One day as I hopped in the old Rambler to go to work, I put it in "R" to get out of the driveway...but it didn't "R". So I put it in "D"...but it wouldn't "D" either. The old faithful Rambler just sat there and purred. I assumed it had to be something with the transmission since kicking the tires didn't get it moving. I was right.

Some friends helped me tow it to the transmission expert. He checked it out and gave me the bad news. The transmission was totally shot...no other option but to buy a new one. I asked the urgent question, "How much?" The news wasn't good there either. A new transmission back then went for the gargantuan price of $180 bucks.

"180 dollars? ", I yelled! "I'm in college, I got a family...I don't have 180 cents, let on a 180 dollars." But my appeal didn't draw any sympathy. "No skin off my back", said the expert, "If you want it fixed, it's $180". So I did the honorable thing, I towed the sick old Rambler back home and kicked the tires again, this time in disgust.

I announced the bad news to my wife who was knee deep in sweat from folding diapers in the hot, non air-conditioned, roach infested mansion we were renting. Our three little girls weren't smiling either. So I tried to get the Rambler running again. No success. It wouldn't "D" or "R". It was dead in the water. We were shipwrecked. No sail, no rudder, no movement, no nothing.

That's when the wife suggested, "If God can heal souls and God can heal bodies, don't you imagine that He could heal a Rambler transmission?" Hmmmm....you don't suppose.....?

That's when one big guy, a cute wife, and three little girls were seen laying their hands on the hood of a 1964 Rambler, with heads bowed as our family agreed in prayer.... "God, please heal our transmission. Amen". Then the miracle happened...God showed up.

Back in the Rambler I crawled, put the key in the ignition and started the engine. Then I put the lever in "D". The Rambler lunged forward like it was supposed to do! I put the lever in "R". The Rambler went backward like it was supposed to do! Our Rambler was healed! Once again God had come to the aide of His children. The girls all felt that we should take a test drive and recommended the grueling trip all the way to the ice cream shop. And since we were there they felt it in our best interest to have an ice cream...just to calm the trauma we had been through. Best money I ever spent.

The Rambler lasted all the time we remained in school and even after we returned home to Ohio where we later traded it in for another used car. It wouldn't surprise me if that old Rambler passed us up one day heading somewhere north on I-75, still with the same transmission.

And then there's the time God miraculously healed an old Ford way out west on highway I-70, that time on the electrical system that had us totally shipwrecked, sitting on the side of an interstate without any help. But that's another story for another time.

These were not the only times that God came to our family's rescue in a miraculous way. The list of God's interventions in seeing to our physical and financial needs is a long one that spans throughout our life. We've moved around the country, lived in almost every conceivable situation,

207

experienced both the good and the tough times...yet our needs were always supplied. We've witnessed God's miracles with all kinds of financial need, yet financial and physical help are not the only things that God has provided for us. He also has delivered us from imminent danger on various occasions, one of which I include in this writing.

GOD'S MIRACULOUS DELIVERANCE
FROM A REBEL GANG

During the time when I was in college in Houston, Texas there were certain sections of the downtown area where you did not want to find yourself late at night, especially alone. But there I was, alone in a deserted, dark alleyway, separated from my friends in the late, late hours of the night...or wee, wee hours of the morning (whichever).

It isn't important what we were doing there at that time of night or how I became separated from my friends, other than to say that we weren't there for any illegal or immoral reasons.

Suddenly a gang of men surrounded me. Each had a knife in one hand and a bottle of liquor in the other. The look on their faces told my fate even before they began to speak. I had never before, or since then, seen such hatred in human eyes. I was a dead man. I would not leave that alleyway alive.

One of the men stood nose to nose with me, reeking of sweat and alcohol...and hate. I actually smelled his animosity and loathing toward me although I had never before met the man. His eyes glared into mine as he challenged me with a simple invitation ..."Talk to me, man". I heard the snickers and laughter from the others as they anticipated what they were about to do.

I began to talk. To this day I have no idea what I said or how long I spoke, but amazingly I had no fear. As I began to speak an awesome miracle took place. The presence of God came down like an invisible protective shield all around me.

God's presence was so evident that the expression on the men's faces began to change. They began to mellow and slump like little kittens. Their eyes no longer glared with defiance and hatred, but were now filled with tears as they began to cry. They backed away a few steps to give me room to speak. Their knives and liquor had dropped to the ground. Their jaws had sagged, their mouths wide open in total amazement.

Something miraculous was happening beyond human capacity or understanding. The love of God was being poured into their hearts from heaven itself. It was probably the first time any of them had ever been exposed to God's presence where perfect love is manifested. In just a few moments of time God changed those violent men from potential murderers to passive spectators of His presence. Rather than putting a knife into my flesh they each put their hands out to shake mine.

Their last words to me were something to the effect that "they had never before witnessed anything like what had just happened ...that I had something they didn't and that they would be giving serious thought to what they heard and witnessed that night." With that they left. I got a hunch I'll see a couple of those guys in heaven some day.

The love of God was so powerful in that Houston alleyway that it caused the most defiant agents of hate to surrender to it. I witnessed how hardened, militant men must succumb to the love of God and how that God protects His children even in the most perilous of circumstance. Yes, I know that the disciples of Christ, including the apostle Paul, all gave their lives for their testimony. There have been many throughout history who were tortured and persecuted for their faith...but there have also been great times of deliverance as in that Houston alleyway...for whatever reason God so willed.

I was delivered from certain death because God once again visited with me. He wasn't quite done with my life yet.

There have been other experiences of God's protective grace that delivered me from danger and death...each of which serves as a certain reminder to me that the promise of God stands true... "I will never leave or forsake you, but will go with you to the ends of the earth".

I can't imagine going through life without Him. Our family is deeply grateful for the visits of God and for His many interventions in our behalf for healing, for protection, for provision and for deliverance. Yet none compares with the profound miracle that happened to me around 10:00 a.m. on a Friday morning in June, 1965. At that moment I experienced a spiritual miracle that removed the fear and guilt of my sinful past to replace them with a pure peace and joy that remains to this day. In an instant moment of time I became a child of God that started a life-long relationship with a loving Heavenly Father that continues to this day.

At this writing I continue to enjoy the benefits of life and health ...and to experience God's visits and assurance. God meets every need of His children. We can verify with certainty that God is not slack concerning His promises. He will do what He has promised.

Many years ago my wife and I took for ourselves His promise to "Seek first the Kingdom of God and His righteousness and all your needs will be supplied." (Mat 6:33) We did our part and God has certainly done His.

There are numerous other experiences that I would very much like to share with you someday, possibly at another writing or in person. I have learned from my own experiences and the experiences of others, that in matters of financial need, physical need, emotional need, spiritual need and any other need...God is loving and merciful to supply our need beyond what we can ever imagine.

But beyond the many miracles that God is capable and willing to perform in our behalf, the greatest blessing in life is to experience His love and presence. Nothing compares with the privilege of having a personal and intimate relationship with our Creator. Knowing that miracles do happen...that's encouraging. Knowing that miracles can happen for you...that's hope. But knowing the "Miracle Maker"...that's what life is all about.

These personal experiences happened just as I described them. I've learned in my years of fellowship with God that everything in the Bible is true and accurate and that all His promises of an abundant and happy life here on earth are real...even when life's situations are sometimes painful and threatening and challenging.

Life has been very good for me...because of God. I am deeply and humbly grateful for all that the Lord has done in my behalf and in behalf of my family. And the best is yet to come...God has promised that His followers shall someday leave the pain and suffering of this world to live eternally with Him.

Because Jesus lives forever...we shall also live forever in the full and joyous presence of God...where sin, sorrow and pain do not exist. I'm not sure what heaven will be like...but where God is, there shall be peace, righteousness and eternal joy. Heaven is all that this world cannot be. The benefits are worth the trip. I don't want to miss it.

I thank you for taking the time to read this simple account of my experiences with God. It is my prayer that you will receive some hope and strength from something that has been shared. You are an important person to God. He is interested in your life and the things that are happening with you.

Whatever your past has been...it is not as important to God as what your future can be. God is no "respecter of persons"... What He has done for me and for millions of others...He will do for you. My prayers are with you.

Your friend who loves you,

Ken Howard

Dr. Kenneth W. Howard

SO, WHO AM I …

…that I would assume to have some information that could be beneficial to you?

Before we talk about me, let's look at some of my friends who contributed to these studies. When it comes to the topic of "life", there is no one person with all the answers.

I am very fortunate to have access to some of the most brilliant minds and researchers on the planet. Somewhere in these studies I've had to call upon the wisdom of physical scientists, astronomers, biologists, chemists, historians, medical researchers, theologians, mathematicians, behavioral experts… and a lot of common sense.

As for me, I have been a student, counselor and teacher on the topic of life for more years than I wish to admit. The previous chapter identifies my true credentials for this writing, but just in case you need some scholarly and professional certification, here's where I'm coming from.

I attended seven universities, majoring in three disciplines…Business, Theology and Psychology. I am licensed in all 50 states as a "healing professional". I have a private

214

counseling practice where I counsel people (by referral) who have really bad problems. I deal with Corporations in their EAP programs; Police Agencies with stress management; Ministers and Churches with marriage, family and spiritual issues; Social Service groups with psychological and social traumas; etc., etc.

I am expected to identify the problem, sort out all the confusion, suggest a realistic remedy, and encourage those who have been beat down with life. It's a great job!

Then there's this research stuff I have to do. I'm supposed to know a little about everything (so they say). My research background spans physical science, ancient and modern history, sociology, Bible and theology, humanities, physics, biology, chemistry, astrophysics, astronomy, world religions, mental health, philosophy...and elephant jokes.

Of all the research I've done over many years, there is no greater wisdom that has come to my attention than that which is recorded in the book we call the Bible. And I say that as a person who is not a member of any organized religious group.

I lecture and teach to special interest groups around the country. I've taught college classes and have been asked to do a weekly national television broadcast, but I declined.

Then, there's this woman I met in high school and married many years ago. She also helps to keep me straight (since she always gets in the last word)...naturally! And she has the greatest kids and grandkids you would ever want to meet.

Finally, I pray a lot. I've learned that knowledge can be gained through study and experience...but wisdom in how to use that knowledge comes only from our omniscient Creator.

So, what do I do for fun? I got a little woodshop at my house where I make stuff. I'd pilot airplanes more often if the little lady (mentioned above) didn't expect me to keep both feet on the ground. And, yep, I enjoy all the college and professional sports (what guy with hair on his chest doesn't).

But the family always comes first...there's no hobby more important than people...at least for me. That's who I am.

ENDORSEMENTS and ACCOLADES

So far, every member of my family and all our friends who have read the book totally endorse it and give it their thumbs up. Of course, you knew they would, didn't you?

I have not approached my professional colleagues and some high-profile people I know to endorse this book. In all honesty, I don't think endorsements have any value. I've never seen an endorsement in a book that doesn't say something nice ...so what's the point? Must be my southern heritage!

Finally, I am a very honest person who will always tell you the truth as best I understand it.

216

Answers And More

The Book Series

Courtesy Of

Dr. Kenneth W. Howard and Colleagues

We are deeply concerned at the great amount of spiritual and social ignorance in this day of imaginary "intellectual enlightenment". A lack of exposure to scientific, historical and Biblical truth in the developmental childhood years, while being taught false science and moral confusion in the educational system, has distorted the reality of human purpose and value.

Further, the distorted messages of secularist life styles, religious confusion and New Age philosophies have created uncertainty and skepticism toward any religious principles.

As a consequence, the current "enlightened" generation is totally ignorant and unprepared to deal with life in a realistic way. They see human life as a non-value, to develop disrespect for their Creator, for themselves, for other human beings, and for the physical environment in which we are dependent for survival. The results are apparent in every shocking newscast.

For many, hope is lost, while depression and frustration take control. We want to help by sharing some positive reality.

217

FIRST TITLES IN THIS SERIES

Book One

Your Life And Beyond

Who am I? Where did I come from?

Why am I here? Where am I headed?

Book Two

The God Of Creation

Can God be trusted? Does God care what happens to me?

What proof is there that God exists? Who is the real God?

Book Three

True Meaningful Religion

What is religion and being religious? What is spirituality?

Why are there so many different religions? Who is right?

How can I find truth for myself?

How can any religion be trusted after all the evils they've done?

Does a person have to belong to a religion to find God?

Book Four

The Final Days Of Mankind

Is the world really coming to an end?

Haven't prophets predicted the world's end for centuries?

Is the Bible really 100% accurate in prophesying future events?

Has the final pre-sign date now occurred?

What signs are we to look for to the world's end?

Book Five

The Problem Of God And Evil

Who is at fault for all the human suffering?

Where did evil come from?

Why do the good and innocent people suffer?

Why doesn't God do something to help us?

More titles are also coming soon to your bookstores and retail outlets. For more information on how to order any of these titles by mail, write to....

Direction, Inc.

P.O. Box 213

Middletown, Ohio   45042

E-Mail: direct@siscom.net

website: http://www.answersandmore.com

Bibliography

The references for this study are so extensive that a listing of all of them would be impractical and would require this book to be twice the size that it is.

You may obtain a complete list of references by written request to:

Kenneth W. Howard, PhD

Direction, Inc.

PO Box 213

Middletown, Ohio   45042

For a partial list, you may visit our website at:

http://www.answersandmore.com